YORK NOTES

Lord of
the Flies

Sir William Golding

Notes by S. W. Foster

Longman   York Press

FOR GILL

YORK PRESS
322 Old Brompton Road, London SW5 9JH

ADDISON WESLEY LONGMAN LIMITED
Edinburgh Gate, Harlow,
Essex CM20 2JE, United Kingdom
Associated companies, branches and representatives throughout the world

First published 1997

ISBN 0-582-31403-8

Designed by Vicki Pacey, Trojan Horse
Illustrated by Anthea Toorchen
Map by Martin Ursell
Typeset by Pantek Arts, Maidstone, Kent
Phototypeset by Gem Graphics, Trenance, Mawgan Porth, Cornwall

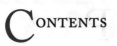ONTENTS

PREFACE

York Notes are designed to give you a broader perspective on works of literature studied at GCSE and equivalent levels. We have carried out extensive research into the needs of the modern literature student prior to publishing this new edition. Our research showed that no existing series fully met students' requirements. Rather than present a single authoritative approach, we have provided alternative viewpoints, empowering students to reach their own interpretations of the text. York Notes provide a close examination of the work and include biographical and historical background, summaries, glossaries, analyses of characters, themes, structure and language, cultural connections and literary terms.

If you look at the Contents page you will see the structure for the series. However, there's no need to read from the beginning to the end as you would with a novel, play, poem or short story. Use the Notes in the way that suits you. Our aim is to help you with your understanding of the work, not to dictate how you should learn.

York Notes are written by English teachers and examiners, with an expert knowledge of the subject. They show you how to succeed in coursework and examination assignments, guiding you through the text and offering practical advice. Questions and comments will extend, test and reinforce your knowledge. Attractive colour design and illustrations improve clarity and understanding, making these Notes easy to use and handy for quick reference.

York Notes are ideal for:

- Essay writing
- Exam preparation
- Class discussion

The author of these Notes is S.W. Foster B.Ed., M.A. (Ed.) who qualified in 1974 and has taught English in the state comprehensive system (11–16) since that time. He lives with his wife and three teenage children in Wiltshire.

The text used in these notes is the Faber and Faber edition, first published in 1958.

Health Warning: **This study guide will enhance your understanding, but should not replace the reading of the original text and/or study in class.**

PART ONE

INTRODUCTION

HOW TO STUDY A NOVEL

You have bought this book because you wanted to study a novel on your own. This may supplement classwork.

- You will need to read the novel several times. Start by reading it quickly for pleasure, then read it slowly and carefully. Further readings will generate new ideas and help you to memorise the details of the story.
- Make careful notes on themes, plot and characters of the novel. The plot will change some of the characters. Who changes?
- The novel may not present events chronologically. Does the novel you are reading begin at the beginning of the story or does it contain flashbacks and a muddled time sequence? Can you think why?
- How is the story told? Is it narrated by one of the characters or by an all-seeing ('omniscient') narrator?
- Does the same person tell the story all the way through? Or do we see the events through the minds and feelings of a number of different people?
- Which characters does the narrator like? Which characters do you like or dislike? Do your sympathies change during the course of the book? Why? When?
- Any piece of writing (including your notes and essays) is the result of thousands of choices. No book had to be written in just one way: the author could have chosen other words, other phrases, other characters, other events. How could the author of your novel have written the story differently? If events were recounted by a minor character how would this change the novel?

Studying on your own requires self-discipline and a carefully thought-out work plan in order to be effective. Good luck.

Two important elements of Golding's life (1911–93) and experience are powerfully reflected in *Lord of the Flies* – his pessimism after the end of the Second World War and his insight, drawn from his life as a schoolmaster, into the way children behave and function.

Born in Cornwall, the son of a schoolmaster, William Gerald Golding attended Marlborough Grammar School before going up to Brasenose College, Oxford, to study sciences. Against his parents' wishes he changed, in his second year at university, to follow the course in English Literature. On leaving he entered the teaching profession, where he remained until he enlisted in the Royal Navy at the start of the Second World War (1939–1945), during which he had a distinguished career, being promoted to commander and seeing action which was to shock him into questioning the horror of war. These experiences inform his writing; he was appalled at what human beings can do to one another, not simply in terms of the Holocaust and other wartime atrocities, but in their being innately evil.

He returned to teaching in 1945 at Bishop Wordsworth School in Salisbury, Wiltshire. Although he wrote and pursued other interests, his writing alone was not enough to sustain him; he wrote chiefly for pleasure. The publication of *Lord of the Flies* (1954) did not release him from teaching, in financial terms, until 1962.

He continued to write, *The Inheritors* (1955), *Pincher Martin* (1956) and *Free Fall* (1959) being the most notable of his novels. The Royal Society of Literature honoured him with a Fellowship in 1955, he was presented with the Nobel Prize for Literature in 1983 and later knighted.

He lived for most of his life in Wiltshire with his wife and two children. He died in 1993.

Historically, the post-war period was one of hope and optimism, but the events which Golding had witnessed did not allow him to see things so simplistically. The war alone was not what appalled him, but what he had learnt of the natural- and original-sinfulness (see Literary Terms) of mankind did. It was the evil seen daily as commonplace and repeated by events it was possible to read in any newspaper which, he asserted, were the matter of *Lord of the Flies*. The war could be regarded as the catalyst which released an already present evil. People possessed this trait in a fundamental and permanent fashion – it could emerge at any time and under any conditions.

It was not just adults who had the capacity for brutality such as that seen in the German labour camps or in Japanese prisons. Golding isolates young children on the island in *Lord of the Flies* and allows us to see them acting with just as much barbarism as is revealed in the adult world. They are, in essence, innocent but nevertheless budding adults – and so potentially evil and sadistic. Children, it is said, can be cruel and in this novel we see stark examples of their cruelty.

It is no accident that Jack and his choir come from a particularly rigid school background. Choir schools are by their nature elitist – probably every bit as much as the more severe public/private schools. The organisation the boys were most familiar with would have been hierarchical, ordered and strict. Beatings, by boys and by masters, would have been commonplace. Without that strict regime and following such past conditioning, it is perhaps not surprising that Jack's deeper self is released in the way we witness.

Not all of the boys are from this culture, however, but the manner and tone of the boys is common in some marked respects. Their language (see Language &

Style) and to some extent their behaviour, is reminiscent of 1940s and 1950s comic books. Heroes like Roy of the Rovers and figures of fun like Frank Richards's Billy Bunter have clearly influenced the way in which Golding portrays the boys. They are initially at least similarly fun loving, possessed of boyish good humour and a sense of natural decency. All of this is to change. Notice too, how their language – even under extreme provocation – is relatively mild. It is also worth considering, in terms of culture and comparison, how a similar group of 1950s girls might have behaved in the same conditions and environment.

Another point of interest is Golding's choice of an island. By its nature it is isolated; there is no outside influence and nothing to distract the boys from their true natures. The island is self-sufficient and self-contained. It is a tropical Garden of Eden, complete with serpent.

PART TWO

SUMMARIES

GENERAL SUMMARY

Chapters 1–4   The story is set on a fictitious tropical island. The
Arrival and   characters are all boys – aged between five and twelve –
exploration   who are the sole survivors of an air crash which takes
place during their evacuation from England.

As the story begins two of the boys, Ralph and Piggy,
are seen searching for the others. They find a large
shell, or conch, which can be blown like a trumpet.
Ralph uses it. At the sound, other boys come in answer
to the call, including a group of choir boys headed by
Jack. Ralph is chosen as leader in preference to Jack,
who is allowed to command his choir as hunters. Ralph
takes Jack and Simon with him to explore the
countryside.

They find that they are on an island which has no sign
of human activity or habitation. However, they think it
is a good island and it has plenty of fruit and pigs, so
they will not starve. They decide to build a fire to draw
attention from passing ships which could rescue them.
The fire is lit using Piggy's spectacles as a magnifying
glass. The wood is so dry that the nearby forest catches
fire; sadly, a little boy with a birthmark, who was
present at the meeting, disappears. Jack offers his
choir/hunters as labour to keep the rescue fire going,
but he becomes increasingly obsessed with the hunting
of the pigs.

As time passes the boys become used to the island.
Ralph continues to worry about the fire and Jack
becomes even more enthusiastic about pig hunting.
While Jack is out hunting, Ralph thinks he can see
smoke from a ship's funnel. He rushes to the signal fire,

only to find that it has gone out. Meanwhile, Jack returns from his first successful hunt to be rebuked for letting the fire go out. In his guilt, he punches Piggy, breaking one lens of his glasses. The boys cook the pig and, in celebration of their hunt, they retell and act out the event.

Chapters 5–8
Beasts of
darkness

In his despair at missing the ship, Ralph decides to call a serious meeting – not one which is light hearted and as disordered as usual. The boys gather in the darkness to listen to what he has to say. Ralph outlines some practical details of life on the island, including the necessity of keeping the fire going, the need for fresh water and shelters and he lastly explains that only one part of the island should be used as a toilet.

He insists on these rules because he is their chief. He then touches on another matter, about which he allows them to give their views – 'the beast'. The discussion ranges from logical dismissals of the idea to almost mindless panic about what the beast is and what form it might take. The meeting breaks up. Ralph considers stepping down as chief and wishes for a sign of some sort from the outside world.

A sign does arrive in the form of a dead airman who descends in a parachute. He lands in the darkness near to the twins, Sam and Eric, who neither see nor hear him very clearly, but describe him quite graphically to the other boys as being the beast. The group decides that the beast must be hunted and might be found in the only part of the island that Jack has not explored. Leaving Piggy to look after the smaller boys, they go off to the tail end of the island but find nothing except an outcrop of rock which would make a good fort.

They decide to go back to the mountain to light the fire even though some of the boys wish to stay and play.

On their way they encounter a pig but are unable to kill it. As they travel back along the coastline it gets late. Simon offers to go back to Piggy and some of the other boys also decide to return to camp soon after. This leaves Ralph, Jack and Roger who determine to go to the mountain – where the beast was last seen. Like Sam and Eric, they see something vaguely in the darkness which frightens them and they run away.

In telling their tale about the beast, Jack is insulted by Ralph's comment that his hunters would be ineffective against it. A meeting is called at which Jack tries to be voted in as chief. He is unsuccessful for a second time and storms off to set up on his own. Other boys gradually join him through the day and they kill a pig, leaving its head as a gift for the beast. Simon is in the forest during the kill and talks with the head of the pig as if it understands him. Later he falls unconscious.

Chapters 9–12
Death and
discovery

Simon wakes up; he is certain that the truth about the beast is to be found on the mountain. He finds the body of the pilot. Meanwhile, Jack's group have moved to another camp. Piggy and Ralph visit them to have some meat. The celebration dance becomes violent just as Simon arrives with news of the airman and he is killed.

At this point there are two distinct groups – the conch group led by Ralph and the savages led by Jack. In the night Jack raids the conch group and steals Piggy's glasses. Ralph goes to the fort to demand that Piggy's glasses be returned. Roger levers a huge rock on to the path which knocks Piggy into the sea and kills him. At the same time, Sam and Eric are captured by the savages and Ralph chased away.

Ralph hides in the jungle but eventually returns to learn from Sam and Eric that he is going to be hunted the

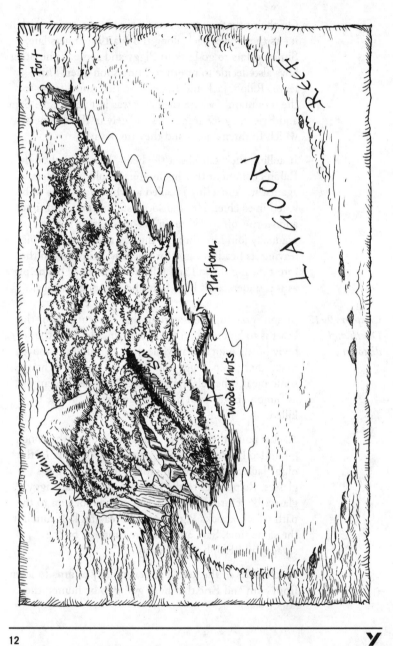

next day. He wakes to the sound of the hunters who roll
two more rocks into the bushes in order to flush him
out. They try setting fire to the area and he runs away
in terror. In his panic he tries desperately to think in a
logical fashion – as Piggy has taught him – but finds it
almost impossible. Eventually he realises that the only
option open to him, if he is to avoid death, is to flee.
Breaking out of the undergrowth, he makes for the
beach but, exhausted, he stumbles and falls.

Instead of the expected death blows, he looks up to the
puzzled gaze of a Royal Navy officer who has seen the
smoke and come to rescue the boys. The officer
expresses surprise at the news that two of the boys are
dead without appreciating the full horror of life on the
island. Far from the romanticised (see Literary Terms)
ideal of *The Coral Island* with all its potential for boyish
adventures, the island has been a backdrop for brutality
and evil.

C HAPTER I – THE SOUND OF THE SHELL

Note the contrasting appearance and attitude of Ralph and Piggy.

During evacuation following a period of hostility in England, a group of boys find themselves marooned on an island. Two of the boys, Ralph and Piggy, are struggling through the island's undergrowth, anxious after their sudden arrival to find adult help and fellow passengers. They appear dazed and confused about what eventually happened to the plane. As yet, they have found no one except each other.

Ralph is clearly more relaxed about the situation than Piggy, taking the opportunity to go for a swim in the tropical heat. Piggy attempts to make Ralph's acquaintance, confiding to him that Piggy is a nickname (that he would prefer was kept a secret), along with other information about his background. In a lagoon Ralph spots a shell which Piggy immediately identifies as a 'conch'. He tutors Ralph in how to blow it in order to make a sound to call the other survivors.

Try to keep a list of the boys who are named.

As the sound of the conch booms across the island, boys begin to emerge slowly. They include a line of choirboys in strange attire. On arrival at the meeting place, one of the boys – Simon – collapses from the heat. The head chorister – Jack Merridew – ignoring his fainted companion, enquires if there are any adult survivors. When he discovers that there are not, he suggests that they fend for themselves. Piggy agrees and proposes that they make a list of names – he has already made a start – but Jack ridicules his list as being 'Kid's names ... Why should I be Jack? I'm Merridew' (p. 22). Clearly not keen to be on first name terms, he criticises 'Fatty' for being too talkative and is corrected by Ralph who says the fat boy's name is Piggy.

When the laughter has faded, Jack says they ought to think about being rescued. Ralph feels they need a chief – a role which Jack, arrogantly, assumes for himself despite the fact that, as Piggy points out, <u>Ralph called the meeting using the conch.</u>

Consider Ralph's choice of Jack and Simon as his exploring companions.

After a vote, Ralph is elected leader or 'chief' (p. 24) and, diplomatically, concedes that Jack is still responsible for the choir – who might double as an army or hunters. Ralph selects Jack and Simon to accompany him, in order to discover whether they are indeed on an island or just a promontory of land.

Before the boys leave, Piggy remonstrates with Ralph about telling the group that his name was 'Piggy'. Ralph apologises and gives Piggy the task of taking the boys' names.

Build up your own mental picture of the island.

Ralph, Jack and Simon tackle the job of exploration with boyish enthusiasm, eventually discovering that they really are on a picturesque, tropical island, complete with lagoon, reefs, mountain and jungle. On their return they find a piglet caught in the creepers. Jack draws his knife to kill it, but cannot do so.

COMMENT

The initial impact of the first chapter in any novel is important – it should be full of possibilities and encourage you to anticipate and predict what might happen later. Many Shakespeare plays contain within the first act all the information and ingredients for later action. The same is sometimes true of prose (fiction). Although your predictions may not be right, you may be able to trace later events back to a point which might explain the reasons behind an action or type of behaviour.

Note when characters first appear.

The descriptions of the principal characters are intended to conjure up an impression in your mind. It is helpful either to make a pencil note in your text (if that is permitted!) or jot down in a notebook the point at which a character is first described and any details you feel may be relevant about them.

Golding creates a clear, early contrast between Ralph and Piggy. The character of Jack is also strongly drawn. Simon features in relatively small but nevertheless significant ways. Pay particular attention to these four characters as they emerge.

The island setting is described in vivid, physical terms. It is clearly a tropical paradise. Notice the words the author uses to portray its richness and variety – reef, cirque, scar, lagoon, defile. It may help to look back at the text and use the information to sketch a simple map (see pages 10, 13, 30 and 31). Notice as you read the book that the island is one of many contrasts – high and low, rocky and forested, friendly and unfriendly. It is also 'roughly boatshaped' (p. 31) – tapering towards one end.

Continuing the idea of first principles, an author does not choose characters or setting purely by chance – they all have a deliberate function. Similarly the names given to the boys are of some significance, albeit slight. Most of the boys have names which were common and popular before and just after the Second World War. Piggy is so named because of his appearance – we never know his true name. Only two names are of Biblical origin or Saint's names. These are Simon (the apostle who carried Christ's cross and was later martyred) and John (a common form of which is Jack).

GLOSSARY   **Home Counties** the central counties of England, generally those closest to London

windbreaker jacket or anorak

hambone frill ruff or collar

Gib. Gibraltar, site of an important British naval base

Addis Addis Ababa in Ethiopia

Wacco...Wizard (*slang*) exclamations of delight →

CHAPTER 2 – FIRE ON THE MOUNTAIN

The three explorers return and Ralph blows the conch to call the other boys to the meeting platform. Uncertainly at first, then with growing confidence, he explains that they are on an uninhabited island. They have found no evidence of any human presence – however slight.

Ralph gradually becomes a leader.

Jack stresses the logical need, as he sees it, for hunters, particularly as they have found pigs which could provide them with meat. Ralph continues to explain more pressing points, firstly that whoever holds the conch is empowered to speak – so that discussions remain orderly.

Second, as there are no adults the boys must fend for themselves. Ralph also reassures the boys that they will be rescued but, as no one knows exactly where they are, this could take a while. The island is one that can provide for their needs so they can survive comparatively easily and also have some fun in the meantime.

During the meeting a six year old boy with a birthmark asks diffidently, through Piggy, what they intend doing about 'a beastie' or 'snake thing' he has seen (p. 39).

ARRIVAL AND EXPLORATION

Ralph says there would not be any such thing on an island of this size. The other boys dismiss the little boy's claims as a dream or his imagination brought on by seeing the creepers. Jack, claiming the conch, says he and his group will ensure that there is not a snake when they go hunting.

Ralph shows his simple faith in the fact that they will be rescued – but could help the process by lighting a fire to produce smoke to attract a passing ship. This idea appeals to the boys, fulfilling both their wish for rescue and their natural lust for fun and adventure. They rush off up the mountain to gather wood. Piggy follows reluctantly, disgusted by their lack of order and foresight. The boys work energetically to gather a pile of wood, but see no way of lighting it. Jack happens on the idea of using Piggy's glasses to magnify the rays of the sun. The wood is dry and rotten, so a flame is quickly kindled.

Contrast the enthusiasm for the fire with the remorse about its destructive effects. The boys continue to feed the fire, producing not signal smoke but flame. They decide to put on green branches to make smoke and determine to keep the fire going – Jack offering his choir/hunters to work in rotation at the task.

Unfortunately, the fire rages out of hand, burning through a large swathe of forest. Piggy becomes firstly frightened at the power that has been unleashed in the fire, then angry at the boys' stupidity and lack of foresight. He also expresses concern for the welfare of the smaller boys – 'the littluns' – and counters Ralph's rebuke at his lack of ability to collect their names by saying that they just keep running off.

Pointing out their lack of care for the island's population of boys, Piggy cites the example of the little boy with the birthmark – who is nowhere to be found. The boys feel guilt and shame at his possible fate.

Y

COMMENT   The fire has two purposes – it is a practical aid to the
           boys' rescue and a source of fun. Under normal
           circumstances boys between 6 and 12 years of age
           would not be entrusted with fire, even with adult
           supervision, and certainly not on this scale. Notice how
           the atmosphere changes when the fire becomes not fun
           but fatal.

           Piggy supports Ralph in this chapter. Ralph has
           explained their predicament and suggests the idea of
           the fire, but even he does not follow the idea through.
           It is Piggy who explains the need for smoke not flame.
           There is a glib irony (see Literary Terms) in the fact
           that although his sight is poor ('Jus' blurs, that's all.
           Hardly see my hand' (p. 45)) his foresight (perception
           and understanding of the consequences of actions) is
           excellent. Further, while the boys see the potential for
           enjoyment in the fire, Piggy sees its potential dangers.
           His manner and tone in this chapter are almost parental
           ('My! You've made a big heap, haven't you?' (p. 44)). He
           also urges the need for practical considerations, like
           shelters, after the cold of the previous night.

           The fears about the beastie/snake thing are rejected
           wholesale by the boys but nevertheless plant a seed of
           apprehension. Observe how this reservation grows in
           the later chapters.

GLOSSARY   **Whee-oh! ... Bong! ... Doink!** (*slang*) exclamations of delight at
           the punishment given to wrongdoers
           Treasure Island ... Swallows and Amazons ... Coral Island
           adventure books by Robert Louis Stevenson, Arthur Ransome
           and R.M. Ballantyne respectively
           Queen Queen Elizabeth II was crowned monarch of England in
           1953, the year before *Lord of the Flies* was published
           Psss an example of onomatopoeia (see Literary Terms); the
           sound of the bow and arrow when used as a fire-making device

y

Arrival and exploration

Chapter 3 – huts on the beach

Jack is totally absorbed by tracking the pigs.

The chapter begins with Jack tracking pigs through the undergrowth. He uses all of his senses but, even with this heightened awareness, when he gets close enough his attempt at a kill is unsuccessful. He gives up after his abortive efforts and returns to the lagoon.

Ralph is similarly preoccupied, building a shelter with Simon's help. Their labours are clearly as unproductive as Jack's hunting. The other boys, including Jack's hunters, have disappeared to swim, eat or play and have given very little assistance.

Why is Jack so keen for meat on an island rich in fruit and shellfish?

Ralph is rather scathing about Jack's failure to get meat and is bitter about the lack of help with the shelters. He resents the time he has put in trying to build them in order that the boys have protection if it rains – and from the 'beast'.

Ralph and Jack dismiss the idea of the 'beastie' as ridiculous. Jack, however, admits to feeling some fear when he is hunting, saying that he feels as if he is being hunted himself. Ralph says that the best way to avoid fear of any sort is to get rescued and repeats the importance of the fire. Jack, on the other hand,

Ralph and Jack are being drawn in to their separate obsessions.

continues to express his enthusiasm for hunting the pigs and obtaining meat. He reasons that the pigs must shelter from the heat of the day on the flatter part of the island. Jack's unceasing fascination with the pigs irritates Ralph. He feels he is doing something out of necessity while Jack is doing something for fun. Ralph complains that he only has Simon's help.

During their discussion Simon – who, it seems, is always around – has wandered off, supposedly to go for a swim. Ralph and Jack go to the bathing pool. Simon has walked along the beach and up the scar. Urged by some of the younger boys to pick fruit from the higher branches, he helps them. Leaving the boys to eat, Simon goes off into the jungle on his own.

COMMENT

Why is Jack obsessed with hunting?

Why is Jack intent on hunting and killing the pigs? Is it because of a sense of failure that he did not kill one immediately when he came across it during the exploration? Details of sight, sound and smell are conveyed strongly in the early part of this chapter. Look again at pages 52–3 in order to understand how the task gets the full focus of Jack's attention.

Ralph is concerned with practical matters – mainly the fire and constructing the shelters. His actions follow the dictates of the assembly, while virtually everyone else is doing what they want. This indicates something about his sense of responsibility and concern for the overall welfare of the boys on the island. Unfortunately, his shelter building has been no more successful than Jack's hunting.

Despite the disparaging comments about the 'beast', even Jack admits to understanding the notion of fear.

At this stage, the fire is still seen as being of importance. Fire is an essential part of any possible rescue. As the story progresses watch how certain characters consider it vital whilst for others it becomes gradually less important. Some of the boys are interested only in things of immediate significance and some merely subsist, that is live from day to day and have no view of future events or prospects.

Piggy is, perhaps surprisingly, not in evidence in this chapter. He is seen in the next chapter as someone who, in Ralph's eyes, is not a worker and so may have avoided any involvement in the shelter building.

We learn more about Simon.

Again Simon plays a part in this chapter and we learn further information about him. He is repeatedly referred to as being strange in one way or another, but exactly what form this takes is never very certain. He is helpful in building the shelters and finding food for the 'littluns' but also content to sit alone in the forest. The younger boys follow him about, which seems to show that he is popular in spite of Ralph's view of him as an oddity.

GLOSSARY   **batty ... Crackers** lunatic, foolish

He's queer. He's funny He's odd or unusual. These words, like the next phrase, may lead to some confusion because of the contemporary use of the words. They simply express Ralph's regard for Simon as being different

delightfully gay and wicked Simon's eyes are 'gay' in the old sense of being happy

CHAPTER 4 – PAINTED FACES AND LONG HAIR

The boys have become almost used to the rhythm of the tropical day – and the mirages produced by the heat – but the pattern of life they are most familiar with prevents them from accepting this new rhythm completely. The boys are described as falling into three broad categories: the 'biguns' (Ralph, Jack, Piggy and Simon), graduating through a vague middle region (which includes Robert and Maurice) to the 'littluns'. This last group – of around six years of age – are denoted as being tanned, dirty, afflicted with stomach problems and prone to nightmares. They spend their time eating, sleeping or playing absorbedly.

Events in the book are often mirage-like and unclear.

Roger's cruelty is mimicked by Maurice.

Three littluns – Henry, Percival and Johnny – are portrayed during one of their games. Roger and Maurice pass them, destroying their sandcastle and kicking sand in Percival's eye. The older boys, it seems, feel only a tinge of guilt. Percival recovers, only to have his younger companions repeat the cruelty.

Roger watches all this and continues his observation as Henry wanders away and becomes fascinated by some minute, transparent sea creatures brought in by the surf.

Roger teases him by throwing stones to land close while he, Roger, is concealed behind a tree.

Jack changes when he puts on the 'mask'.

Jack arrives, having found some clay to use as facial camouflage, and explains that he believes the pigs see him rather than smell his scent. He smears his face and goes off to hunt.

At the bathing pool Ralph considers Piggy in a negative light and recognises him to be an outsider and an irritation. Suddenly, Ralph believes he can see the smoke from a ship's funnel. He gets badly scratched as he dashes through the undergrowth in an effort to get to the signal fire – only to discover that it has gone out. Ralph shouts to the disappearing ship in an expression of his total despair.

Ralph's despair contrasts with Jack's jubilation.

The hunters return, chanting in triumph having killed a pig. Ralph, at odds with the torrent of enthusiasm, states that the signal fire was out when there was a ship passing. Eventually, Jack realises the futility of hunting against the possibility of rescue. Unable to face the barrage of supporting comments from Piggy, he punches him, breaking one lens of his glasses.

Jack apologises grudgingly for letting the fire go out; it is then relit, using the only remaining lens in Piggy's spectacles. The boys cook the pig and Ralph is forced out of his silence to accept some meat. Piggy asks for some but Jack points out that he is not entitled to any because he did not hunt. Simon, guilty at not having hunted either, gives his meat to Piggy. Jack is infuriated at this apparent ingratitude shown towards his hard work and generosity. He glories in retelling the story of the hunt and some of boys re-enact the kill, in primitive style. Ralph, unable to come to terms with their failure to contact the ship, decides to call a meeting.

COMMENT   In the early part of this chapter patterns of behaviour
          have become settled – the routine of the day; the way
          the boys have become pigeon-holed into groups and
          initial impressions of the characters are now crystallised.

          On the other hand, elements of that same behaviour are
          magnified and enlarged as the chapter progresses. A
          gradual de-civilisation is emerging. Evidence of this can
          be seen in the lack of cleanliness over eating and
          personal hygiene. The same deterioration is noticeable
          in the way that Roger's unkindness is copied by
          Maurice and then repeated by the littluns. Although
          Maurice feels some shame at his actions, he quickly
          forgets about what he has done because there are no
          adults present to punish him. Finally, the hunters'
          response to their successful kill is both primitive and
          pagan complete with tribal dance, tri-syllabic chanting
          (see Literary Terms) and a simplistic replay of the
          whole event.

          The characteristics of Ralph and Jack are further
          developed in this chapter. Jack is determined and
          single-minded in his pursuit of the pigs yet proud and
          pugnacious in the incident involving Piggy. He
          apologises for letting the fire out but not, you will
          notice, for breaking the glasses. He lashes out at Piggy
          partly because he is embarrassed at the truth of his
          omission, but also because he feels cornered. The
          apology is a painful – and unusual – experience for him.

Ralph is feeling   Ralph exhibits real despair at the passing of the ship,
the pressures of   possibly because he is beginning to feel the pressure of
leadership.   his overall responsibility for the boys. He has also been
          involved in work, building the shelters, and the idea
          that the island is fun is wearing thin. As you read the
          next chapter, notice how Ralph's low opinion of Piggy
          ('Piggy was a bore' (p. 70)) alters.

TEST YOURSELF (Chapters 1–4)

A

Identify the speaker.

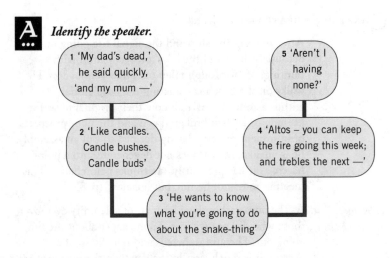

1 'My dad's dead,' he said quickly, 'and my mum —'

2 'Like candles. Candle bushes. Candle buds'

3 'He wants to know what you're going to do about the snake-thing'

4 'Altos – you can keep the fire going this week; and trebles the next —'

5 'Aren't I having none?'

Idenify the person(s) to whom this comment refers.

6 'He's queer. He's funny'

7 He was the only boy on the island whose hair never seemed to grow

Check your answers on page 86.

B

Consider these issues.

a The contrasts between Ralph and Piggy in the first chapter.

b How Jack affects you, the reader, and the boys – most of whom do not vote for him.

c Ralph's view of Piggy before and after the ship is sighted.

d The organisation and tone of the first assemblies.

e How the author conveys Jack's concentration on tracking the pig in particular and hunting in general.

f The nature of Ralph's despair at missing the ship.

g The author's description of the physical features of the island.

h How the differences between Ralph and Jack emerge.

BEASTS OF DARKNESS

CHAPTER 5 – BEAST FROM WATER

After missing the ship and the signal fire going out because of Jack and the boys' preoccupation with hunting, life for Ralph takes on a new seriousness. He walks on the beach considering the boys' initial enthusiasm for the island; how their original ideas for keeping order had broken down and the poor prospects of imminent rescue. Having decided to call an assembly, he is anxious that it does not degenerate into a pointless fiasco, as it has previously. He thinks beforehand, 'This meeting must not be fun, but business' (p. 83).

An important meeting is held.

As the boys gather there is an air of solemnity even over those who did not witness Ralph's anger about the fire going out. The atmosphere is additionally sombre because it is much later in the day than the meetings are usually held. Before starting to speak, Ralph considers the weight of his responsibilities as chief. He recognises the need to be able to think rationally and systematically as important requirements for a leader. He also realises that Piggy has the capacity for clear thinking and begins to regard his fat companion with new-found respect.

Ralph objects to the breakdown in order and cleanliness.

Ralph opens the meeting by setting out ground rules about how it is to be conducted, so that nothing spoils the impact of the few, simple points he wishes to make. In a plain, ordered fashion he raises five issues which he feels are central to their survival and well-being. The first four are practical matters which provoke little discussion or argument. He explains the need for fresh water; the need for shelters to be built; the necessity of using one agreed place as a lavatory and, most important of all, the need to keep the fire going if they are ever to be rescued. As their elected chief, he insists that these rules are adhered to.

The fifth and final item on Ralph's agenda is 'the fear' or 'the beast'. It is the only matter on which he will

allow discussion and, understandably, the only matter
about which many of the boys are unable to express
their feelings. Jack, now regarded as a proven hunter,
discounts the notion of the beast being a real, tangible
creature. Having been all over the island and having
found nothing larger than pigs, he regards the idea as
nonsense. The beast is therefore, he argues, intangible –
a product of the littluns' imagination – and he berates
them for their cowardice. Piggy agrees with Jack, in
part. He too rejects the idea of the beast being a real
thing – using his knowledge of science and natural

Have Piggy's past
experiences made
him fearful of
people?

logic. He also dismisses the notion of the beast being a
creature of the imagination, but does so with sympathy
and understanding. The only fear worth considering is
the fear of people.

At this point one of the littluns comes forward and
admits to having a nightmare and to seeing something
moving about in the forest. It turns out that it could
have been Simon who is then rebuked for frightening
the littluns. Another little boy – Percival Wemys
Madison – is coaxed by Piggy into telling his story.
Unfortunately he ultimately dissolves in tears which
produce near hysteria in the other younger boys. It is
only Maurice's clowning and his return to the subject of
the beast that enables order to be restored. His mention

What might Simon
have said if
allowed to finish
speaking?

of giant squid, however, produces further distress and
Ralph blows the conch for silence. Simon feels the need
to speak and takes the conch but has neither the
language, or the opportunity, to express his notions of
evil. Piggy's attempt to discount the existence of ghosts
is interrupted by Jack and then put to the vote by
Ralph. In the gloom it is difficult to assess the outcome,
but Piggy still insists that ghosts do not exist. Jack's
contempt for Piggy and his lack of respect for the
authority of the conch and Ralph as leader lead him to
disregard the rules. Jack leaves and the assembly breaks

up in disarray. Ralph, Piggy and Simon remain to consider their problems. Ralph contemplates giving up as chief. Piggy fears for his own position if Ralph were to relinquish his title. They all long for adult support and wish they could be sent 'a sign or something' (p. 103), from the outside world. Their thoughts are disturbed by Percival Wemys Madison crying in the darkness.

COMMENT   Although the chapter is called 'Beast from Water', in 'deciding on the fear' (p. 89) a number of explanations are put forward. These range from real wild creatures, like the giant squid, to human beings as a source of fear. Unreal phenomena are also considered – fear created by the imagination, fear of evil and fear of the supernatural in the form of ghosts. Notice how each suggestion is received by the different boys.

The boys start to split into two factions.   This chapter marks the beginnings of a break in the relationship between Ralph and Jack and the division of the boys on the island into two factions. Think about who would be in each group and how they might behave.

CHAPTER 6 – BEAST FROM AIR

Ralph and Simon carry Percival to one of the shelters and eventually they all fall asleep. Ten miles above them a battle is being fought and a 'sign … from the world of grown-ups' (p. 104) comes down in the form of a parachutist. He lands on the mountain where the breeze and the parachute's suspension lines control his body like the strings of a puppet. Sam and Eric have been on duty at the fire but have almost allowed it to go out. In the early morning darkness, while trying to rekindle the fire, Eric hears the sound of the parachute canopy. Neither boy can see very clearly and, believing they have encountered 'the beast', they run away in terror.

Sam and Eric behave, and are regarded as, one person.

They report the sighting to Ralph who, conscious of the near panic of the previous evening, tells them to call an assembly as calmly and quietly as possible. However, Sam and Eric, speaking as one, give a description which is both terrifying – because it is reinforced by duplication – and reassuring – because now it is recognised as real.

Their mention of the beast's teeth and claws, its eyes and the way it 'kind of sat up' (p. 109) leave the other boys in no doubt that the beast is a tangible thing which can, therefore, be hunted.

Jack is ecstatic at the prospect of a hunt but Piggy, for all his dismissal of the fear of ghosts the previous evening, admits to being frightened. He suggests that they stay where they are in the hope that the beast will not come near them. Ralph points out that it would not, therefore, be possible to fetch food and details Piggy to look after the littluns. Piggy takes the conch in order to

Jack questions the authority of the conch – the symbol of democracy.

explain that he is frightened and of little use with his broken glasses. Jack interrupts to ridicule both Piggy's fear and the importance of the conch. He says that the ritual of holding it to speak to the assembly is pointless and unproductive. The atmosphere is tense as Ralph reaffirms the value of the conch and his own leadership by telling Jack to sit down. Ralph then takes control of the situation by saying that the beast leaves no tracks and cannot be hunted in the normal way. He reminds the boys of the importance of rescue as their top priority. They will therefore search for the beast in the tail end of the island – the only part that Jack has not visited – then return to the mountain to re-light the fire.

Leaving Piggy and the littluns behind, Ralph and the bigger boys go in search of the beast with Jack in the lead. As they walk along Simon reflects on his inability to speak to the group about his ideas about the beast.

He then has a vision of the beast as 'a human at once heroic and sick' (p. 113).

Arriving at the tail end of the island, even Jack is apprehensive. Ralph takes the initiative, as leader, to go forward alone, comforted by Simon's reassurance that there is no beast. He discovers nothing but an outcrop of rock which Jack, following shortly after him, says would make an ideal fort. Ralph insists that they return and light the fire on the mountain. Many of the boys want to stay at the fort and play, or roll rocks off the outcrop into the sea, but Ralph forcefully reminds them of the importance of the signal fire. Unwillingly they leave the outcrop, led by Jack.

Ralph is gaining the ability to think like a leader.

COMMENT   Ralph shows a degree of common sense and an almost obsessive determination in this chapter. He attempts, despite the undercurrent of resentment from Jack, to push through some of the points he made during the previous night's assembly. He shows courage in ultimately leading the exploration of the far end of the island and moral courage in facing up to Jack over the supremacy of the conch.

Despite Jack's bravado and Piggy's theorising, neither of them show the courage of their convictions. Jack is keen to hunt the beast but finally cannot do so. Piggy is intellectually convinced that ghosts do not exist but declares his fear of the beast and stays to look after the littluns.

Keep an eye on Simon's actions.

Simon emerges once again as a complex and important minor character. Despite the fact that he says and does comparatively little, his speech and actions are highly significant. Take careful note of what happens whenever his name is mentioned.

The discovery of the outcrop of rock at the end of the island is relevant to later action in the novel. While Jack enthuses about its possibilities as a fort, Ralph senses something evil in the enormity of the ocean which surges around the island at that point. This place is later known as Castle Rock.

CHAPTER 7 – SHADOWS AND TALL TREES

The boys follow Jack along the pig run and the sound of the sea in the afternoon sun allows Ralph to forget the beast. He asks Jack to stop when they come to some fruit trees so that the boys can eat. As they take a break, Ralph considers the filthy state of his shirt and contemplates washing it. He also feels he needs to have a bath and clean his teeth. He is alarmed at the fact that he has resorted to the childish habit of biting his nails and wonders aloud whether he will soon start sucking his thumb. Once again – see pages 83–4 in Chapter 5 – Ralph considers the subject of cleanliness and reviews the state of the other boys. They too are dirty, their hair tangled, their clothing worn and stiff with sweat. Ralph is a little shocked that he now regards these conditions as normal.

Simon shows insight and provides reassurance.

Turning from the boys, Ralph is awed by the immensity and power of the ocean – which he sees as a barrier between the island and the civilised world. Simon, with great insight, correctly interprets Ralph's silent reverie as a longing to return home and reassures him that he will get there, eventually.

Roger discovers some pig droppings and Jack suggests that it would be convenient to hunt the pig at the same time as they were hunting 'the other thing' (p. 123) – the beast. Ralph agrees conceding, in his own mind, that they will eventually get back to the mountain.

As Jack tracks the pig Ralph has time to cast his mind back to the comforts of his typical English, middle-class home. He is jolted out of his reflections by the

Ralph's picture of home contrasts with his fear and insecurity about the island.

sound of a pig. He throws his spear, hitting the boar on the nose and so diverting it. They follow the boar and Ralph, caught up in the excitement of the hunt, prides himself on his achievement, only to be rebuked by Jack – who has sustained a minor injury – for not throwing more effectively.

In retelling his part in the hunt, Ralph inadvertently incites the boys into performing a playful re-enactment of it – complete with chant. Although Robert, who represents the pig, is only slightly hurt, Ralph experiences something of the frenzy and blood lust of the hunters (see Crowd mentality in Themes). Jack suggests getting one of the boys to dress up as a pig and jokes about using the littluns for the purpose.

Ralph raises the subject of going to the mountain and starting the fire, but is reminded that they do not have Piggy's glasses. He proposes that they follow the coastline to the mountain and climb up it through the burnt area. This turns out to be difficult; they encounter impenetrable forest which forces them down to a dangerous course at the cliff edge. Ralph pauses to

Simon shows his concern for the littluns.

consider his wider responsibilities to Piggy and the littluns. Simon volunteers to go back through the forest to them.

Ralph questions Jack about his explorations to find out where they are in relation to the pig run. Jack responds that the pig run is close by, below the mountain. They

Tensions rise between Jack and Ralph about their courage – or lack of it.

decide to push through the forest to get to it. Jack jibes at Ralph for putting off going to the mountain and mocks his cowardice – at which Ralph reminds Jack of his own lack of courage at Castle Rock. When put to the vote, all but Ralph, Jack and Roger decide to return to Piggy at the platform.

The three boys push on through the burnt patch of forest and Jack, perhaps shamed by the reminder of his earlier behaviour, goes on to the mountain top while Ralph and Roger wait in silence. Jack eventually returns, clearly shocked – despite his bravado – by having seen something 'bulge' and 'plop' (p. 134). Ralph leads the boys to the mountain top to see the almost indistinguishable hump which Jack has described. Suddenly, the clouds shift from in front of the moon, the wind roars – so that the parachute moves the body – and the 'creature lifted its head' revealing 'something like a great ape' (p. 136). The boys leave the mountain in haste.

COMMENT   The enactment of the hunt is reminiscent of tribal dances, which are a ritualistic representation of what it is hoped the tribe will experience in a successful hunt in the future. This, coupled with Jack's mask and the rallying chant of earlier chapters, highlights the move away from conventional behaviour.

Jack and Ralph vie with each other, each trying to prove his own courage and right to the leadership. Jack, already resentful of Ralph, must, it seems, achieve the summit of the mountain in order to save face after his apparent cowardice at Castle Rock. Jack has not been quite so thorough in his exploration of the island as he claims.

Ralph is better able to 'think' now; at one point thinking aloud quite unashamedly. The ability to think is openly attributed to Piggy. Ralph recognises that Jack hates him – but does not understand why – with the 'new understanding that Piggy had given him' (p. 130).

Images of nature abound.   Natural images (see Literary Terms) and descriptions abound in this chapter. Ralph's continuing thoughts about the vastness of the sea – see Chapter 6 – are repeated at greater length. The description of the forest is vivid; the undergrowth on one side is impassable, the sea and cliffs on the other are threatening. The final revelation of the beast is effected by natural forces.

BEASTS OF DARKNESS

The dramatic visual image at the end of the chapter with the moon and the wind together conspiring to reveal the beast has a suitably dynamic impact on the three boys.

GLOSSARY   **batty** crazy, silly

Berengaria Berengar/Berengarius of Tours (999–1088) claimed that Communion wine represented – rather than physically became – the blood of Christ. Simon is telling Jack to lick his wound

Windy? Frightened?

CHAPTER 8 – GIFT FOR THE DARKNESS

The boys return and tell about the sighting of the beast. Piggy questions Ralph closely about it and, from Ralph's responses, concludes that they would be powerless against such a creature. Jack counters by saying that it might be tackled by his hunters. Ralph is contemptuous, describing them as 'Boys armed with sticks' (p. 138).

Jack is hurt by Ralph's dismissal of his hunters and blows the conch to call a meeting – which Ralph says he had intended to do anyway.

It is now common knowledge that the three boys have seen the beast. Jack maintains that it is 'a hunter' (p. 139) – although on what evidence is unclear. Ralph, he says, has insulted his hunters; Ralph is not a proper chief and has shown himself to be cowardly. After a brief volley of argument Jack gets to the main thrust of his speech and holds a vote of no confidence in Ralph's leadership. No one votes to remove Ralph as leader so, *Keep notes through* for the second time, Jack is unsuccessful. (On this *the chapter of* occasion, not even the choir vote for him.) In his anger *which boys are in* and frustration at this, Jack walks off in tearful fury to *which group.* set up on his own.

Piggy is relieved at Jack's departure.

Ralph is bewildered by Jack's reaction and feels that he will come back in the evening. Piggy, however, is rather relieved at Jack's departure. He says that there will be no need for Jack and his hunters now, and that the boys must stay near the platform to avoid the beast – about which he is still sceptical. Simon shyly and hesitantly suggests that they should climb the mountain. Typically, the boys ignore him. Piggy brings up the matter of the fire and proffers the suggestion that they light it by the bathing pool instead of on the mountain.

The boys set to build the fire with a sense of purpose, using rather damp wood, and Piggy takes the initiative for once to light it. With the fire lit, Piggy and Ralph consider reorganising things and making a list of names, only to find that many of the boys have drifted away. It is suspected that these, like Jack, were the troublemakers who did not want to 'play'.

Ralph feels that they will be better off on their own. Piggy, Sam and Eric collect some fruit, which is eaten in an atmosphere of celebration. They discover that Simon too has disappeared, they suspect to climb the mountain. He has in fact gone off to sit in solitude.

How does Golding build up the atmosphere during the hunt?

Meanwhile, Jack has gathered a group of boys that he is going to lead as chief. He tells them that they will forget about the beast, kill a pig and have a feast at Castle Rock. The boys move off to the forest to hunt. They find a sow with her piglets and kill her. The atmosphere, both tense and violent, is broken only by Maurice's coarse humour and another – this time amusing – re-enactment of the hunt.

Jack guts the pig and, in his capacity as 'Chief', instructs the boys to take the meat to the platform. He also divulges his plan to raid the other group to get some fire. They put the pig's head on a stick as a gift for the beast and leave the forest to return to the beach.

BEASTS OF DARKNESS

Simon emerges from the undergrowth and approaches the pig's head, communicating with it both verbally and with silent understanding.

Back at the conch group camp, Ralph and Piggy discuss the fire as the thunder clouds gather. The importance of the fire to the boys' rescue is repeated. Ralph broaches the subject of what would happen if they gave up caring about rescue. Just as he is considering the central question of 'what makes things break up like they do?' (p. 154), his thoughts are disturbed by the arrival of the hunters.

Jack invites them to a feast, but this is simply a diversion to allow the raiders to steal some fire. Afterwards Ralph, Piggy, Sam and Eric and Bill consider Jack's offer and the lure of meat, but are not tempted to join the hunters.

What is the matter with Simon? Elsewhere, Simon is still communicating with the Lord of the Flies – the pig's head on a stick – which speaks to him in the voice of a school master. Eventually he falls unconscious.

COMMENT   The split between Jack and Ralph and the establishment of the conch group and the hunters as separate entities could be anticipated. It is a natural development of the differences between the two main characters. The ethos of the conch group is in marked contrast to that of the hunters, who are primarily interested in having fun. The hunters behave in a primitive fashion – wear paint, use spears, are virtually naked and live for the moment. Significantly, they have no conch or other object to regulate who speaks and when. On the contrary, Jack's announcement is reinforced by two hunters in a stylised and rehearsed afterword – 'The Chief has spoken' (p. 155) – which prevents further argument.

The hunters become savages.

Piggy is pleased and relieved at Jack's departure. And not even the choir vote for him. Think about why so many of the boys later join him.

There are references in ancient history to a 'god of the flies' being worshipped by pagan civilisations. Although Jack has said that they are going to forget about the beast, the pig's head is still left as a gift to placate it. There is a grudging acceptance of, and respect for, this unnamed being which has been raised to the status of deity. The pig's head is left as a sacrifice in gratitude for a successful hunt. There is a parallel between the way the boys defer to their 'god' – the Lord of the Flies – and the way that they idolise Jack. He is, in a sense, lord over them – his own flies, or menials.

What is Simon's true nature?

Simon's behaviour raises certain questions. In Chapter 1 it became evident that he is prone to fainting; in Chapter 9 it appears that he is epileptic: 'Simon's fit passed' (p. 160). Are his actions governed by his medical condition? He may be hallucinating. However, his understanding of the Lord of the Flies goes beyond that expressed in normal speech and thought, to an almost spiritual sympathy for the creature.

GLOSSARY

covert copse; group of trees or bushes

flinked flicked or shook

Identify the speaker.

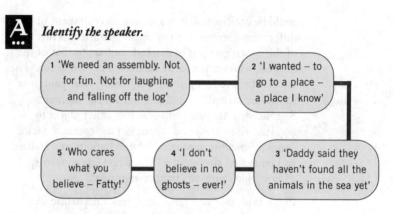

1 'We need an assembly. Not for fun. Not for laughing and falling off the log'

2 'I wanted – to go to a place – a place I know'

5 'Who cares what you believe – Fatty!'

4 'I don't believe in no ghosts – ever!'

3 'Daddy said they haven't found all the animals in the sea yet'

Identify the person(s) to whom this comment refers.

6 Presently he stood up, holding the dripping sow's head in his hands

7 He knew that one of his times was coming on. The Lord of the Flies was expanding like a balloon

Check your answers on page 86.

B **Consider these issues.**

a Ralph's ordering of his thoughts before the assembly.

b The contrasts between the two groups of boys.

c The development of tension in the pig hunt.

d Which symbols are most important to the two groups.

e How the author reveals the beast to us, in its various guises.

f The changes in the behaviour of some of the boys that have occurred since the beginning of the novel.

g How the author shows the passage of time in simple details.

CHAPTER 9 – A VIEW TO DEATH

Simon is lying next to the Lord of the Flies. A storm is brewing, but nothing moves except the flies on the pig's head and intestines. Eventually Simon wakes from his fit, still intent, it seems, on climbing the mountain. His recent experience has left him weak and bloody, his eyes have lost their usual lustre. He staggers up the mountain against the gathering wind.

The beast is now 'harmless and horrible'.

Arriving at the top, he finds the flyblown body of the parachutist. The suspension lines of the parachute create the impression that the body is moving. Simon examines the condition of the rotting corpse and is violently sick. He untangles the parachute lines so that the body is stilled and, observing the new camp the boys have apparently made on the beach, decides, despite his frailty, to return and tell them the news.

Back at the bathing pool Ralph is enjoying the water – even Piggy ventures in. The heat is oppressive as the thunder clouds gather, giving Piggy a headache which makes him yearn for cool rain. The other boys have gone to Jack's camp they believe. Piggy and Ralph decide to visit it to have some meat and, as Piggy says, 'make sure nothing happens' (p. 163). They can hear the boys well before they see them. Jack is the focal point of the camp, surrounded by food and drink, bedecked with leaves and daubed in paint.

The babble of noise drops as the pair enter the camp. The silence is broken by laughter as two boys accidentally burn Piggy with hot meat. Jack dominates the whole group like an imperious monarch – offering meat, ordering drink and extending an invitation to join his tribe.

Jack and Ralph, working together, could have had meat and shelter.

Jack and Ralph vie for leadership; one pressing the value of meat, the other the importance of shelters. The stalemate is broken as the rain starts, by Jack suggesting

Simon stumbles into the dance.

that the boys perform their dance. At first Roger plays the pig, then amid the rising frenzy and chanting he rejoins the hunters, leaving the centre of the circle empty. The littluns start a circle of their own but soon return to the biguns making a large, horseshoe shape. In the climax of chanting, dancing, thunder and lightning Simon emerges from the undergrowth with the news of the dead man on the hill.

His words are ignored as the boys use him as the pig – the victim of their dance – and in the frenzy he is killed.

On the mountain top, the now released parachute carries the body into the sea. As the rain stops the tide washes Simon's body out to sea as well. The stars in the night sky pick out strange, luminous creatures which surround his body with light.

COMMENT

Simon is a prophet.

Simon is determined to reach the top of the mountain where, in a sense, the truth lies – both literally and metaphorically. Simon frees the dead airman, who is then given the dignity of a burial at sea. Simon too is consigned to the sea after his murder. The news of 'a body on the hill' (p. 168) provides a clear piece of Christian imagery (see Literary Terms). Simon can be viewed as a prophet and visionary, with a parallel between the parachutist on the mountain and Christ on the hill at Calvary. The description of the halo of creatures which surround him with light as he floats out to sea is both poignant and significant. The fact that his news is ignored by the boys may also be worth some consideration.

Images of light and dark, clear and opaque, are important throughout the book but are particularly strong in this chapter.

The description of Jack's camp, in which he is set apart as being superior, is in marked contrast to the earlier assemblies with Ralph and the conch. Ralph's meetings were good-natured, inefficient and democratic. Jack's are severely businesslike, authoritarian and even dictatorial.

Piggy shows his concern for others.

Piggy again shows himself to be both parental and protective in his anxiety to visit Jack's camp to 'make sure nothing happens' (p. 163).What do you think he feared might occur? Could even Piggy have anticipated the outcome of the dance? Is it significant that, like Simon, Piggy has a headache just before these dramatic events happen?

CHAPTER 10 – THE SHELL AND THE GLASSES

On the morning after Simon's death, Piggy squints at an approaching figure and recognises him as Ralph who now looks as dishevelled as the rest of the boys. Without actually mentioning Simon, they slowly come

The boys try to eradicate the memory of the previous night.

round to the subject by discussing the need for an assembly. Ralph scoffs at the futility of the conch and talks about Simon and what he now realises was his murder. Piggy sees this admission as negative and unhelpful. He views Simon's death as the product of 'the fear' and 'that bloody dance' (p. 172) – eventually dismissing it as an accident which is best put out of their minds. Ralph and Piggy gradually convince themselves that they had nothing to do with it.

Sam and Eric return from collecting wood; they too deny being present at the feast – although they clearly were.

The camp now set up at Castle Rock is guarded by sentries who challenge Roger. He says he could still climb up to the rock if he wanted to, at which they show him a simple device to deter unwelcome visitors. (There is a lever pushed under the highest rock so that it can be dropped on enemies approaching along the narrow strip of land leading to the camp.) Roger admires the ingenuity of Jack, who he regards as a 'proper Chief' (p. 176). Jack is apparently going to take them hunting. He is also going to punish Wilfred for some vague and undisclosed misdemeanour. Roger considers the consequences of ungoverned power.

Jack gives orders rather than asking for opinions.

Jack, sitting before a semicircle of boys, delivers instructions about the forthcoming hunt and the defence of Castle Rock. He proclaims that the beast – Simon – came in disguise the previous night. The muted suggestion that they killed Simon is emphatically denied by Jack. The beast might come again so they must leave the head of each kill as a gift to keep in favour with it. Their fire has gone out, so Jack plans to visit the other group with Maurice and Roger – keeping to the coastline to avoid the beast.

Ralph tries to relight the fire but the wood is too damp. Together with Piggy, Sam and Eric he contemplates methods of escape should the signal fire not attract rescuers. Eric considers the prospect of being taken prisoner 'by the reds' (p. 179) if they can not get away, and suggests that this might be preferrable to being captured by Jack and his savages. Ralph, tacitly admitting that he was a witness to the murder, reflects on Simon's last words about a dead man on the hill.

Sam and Eric are losing heart.

Another attempt is made to light the fire which yet again proves unsuccessful. Sam and Eric, whether from shock or exhaustion, feel that their efforts are pointless, but Ralph reminds them that the fire is their only hope. However, because it is too dark to collect wood, they leave the fire to be lit the next day.

Again Ralph reflects on life at home.

In the shelter Ralph casts his mind back to the security of home; he imagines the prospect of rescue and the lure and attraction of the civilised world. He drifts into a nightmare, from which Piggy awakes him. Sam and Eric too are troubled and fight together in their sleep. Ralph and Piggy recognise that the strain is affecting all of the boys.

Y

Piggy hears a noise. Suddenly, his name is called and he believes, finally, that the beast is real after all and has come for him. The beast – Jack and his hunters – dives into the shelter and a fight ensues. Ralph pounds viciously into the face of an attacker until his efforts are halted by a knee in the groin, which fells him.

Piggy worries about the conch, not his lost glasses. When the perpetrators have gone the boys take stock of their injuries. Ironically (see Literary Terms), Eric's face is bloody but he prides himself on the fact that he disabled his attacker by striking him between the legs! Piggy is uninjured, but was fearful for the safety of the conch. The hunters, meanwhile, return to Castle Rock – not with the conch but with Piggy's glasses.

COMMENT   This chapter describes the aftermath of Simon's murder. The tone is one of hopelessness and dejection among both the conch group and the savages of Castle Rock. Interestingly both groups, in one way or another, try to brush the incident aside by childishly framed denials. Is it too far-fetched to suggest that the three-fold denial by the boys is an allegory (see Literary Terms) for the Biblical story of Simon Peter denying his knowledge of Christ on three occasions 'before the cock crows'? This aside, it is only Ralph who recognises the death for what it is – murder.

The organisation of Jack's group is significant. Again he is placed in a prominent position with a semicircle of boys around him. As on a previous occasion he is revered and set apart in importance. This contrasts sharply with the assemblies held using the conch, where everybody could speak and, like King Arthur's Round Table, everyone was of equal value. The semicircle or horseshoe seems to invite someone or something to fill the opening it creates. It was into such a void that the hapless Simon stumbled on the previous evening.

There is irony (see Literary Terms) in the misdirected aggression displayed by Ralph and Eric who, it turns out, were fighting each other in the darkness. Could this symbolise (see Literary Terms) the pointlessness of violence used without thought or reason?

It is useful at this point to reflect on what all the boys had experienced over their time on the island – fear, deprivation, discomfort, lack of parental care, illness, intimidation and depression. After all of these comes the heinous crime of murder – a crime of which they are all guilty, in a sense.

The conch and the glasses are symbolic objects.

The chapter is entitled 'The Shell and the Glasses', both of which are symbols. The shell could represent democracy, the voice of reason or decency (see Law and order in Themes). It is of no use in itself beyond being a beautiful object – its use is in what it represents or symbolises to the boys.

The glasses are useful to Piggy, but have a function beyond that for everyone else – they can start the fire. The ability to make fire is something which sets human beings apart from animals. The glasses, therefore, symbolise fire, but also knowledge – enlightenment – and dominion over primitive instincts. It is notable that Piggy perceives the conch as the more valuable; holding it – literally – with respect and affection during the events of the next chapter.

GLOSSARY   **bloody dance** the word 'bloody' is used here as a swear word, but the dance is bloody in another sense because it leads to Simon's death

he asked for it it was his fault, he got what he deserved

reds Communists – presumably the current war was one against a communist country

round the bend ... Bomb happy ... Crackers insane, crazy

pills testicles

CHAPTER 11 – CASTLE ROCK

Early next morning Ralph tries to salvage the beginnings of a fire from the previous day's ashes, but without Piggy's glasses his task is hopeless. As well as no fire, Piggy is virtually sightless without his glasses. He suggests that Ralph calls an assembly. Nobody turns up except Sam and Eric.

Ralph lists Jack's crimes – letting the fire go out; killing Simon and now theft. When asked what he is going to do, Ralph suggests that they approach Jack as a civilised human being, not a savage, and explain the seriousness of being rescued.

What, says Piggy, is the one thing Jack hasn't got?

Piggy, too, feels passionately that Jack should be told how to behave. Gaining his courage from the authority of the conch, he feels Jack should respond out of common decency and respect for the rule of law. Piggy conveys his faith in the ultimate power of the conch in the pride he exhibits at the prospect of carrying it to Castle Rock.

Why are the twins so fearful of the painted faces?

The boys consider tidying themselves up to remind the savages of the civilised world, but abandon the idea. They feel that however they look will be no worse than the appearance of the savages, who will be painted and masked – a thought which the twins find disconcerting. Ralph again repeats the need for smoke, although Piggy has to prompt him as to why it is so essential. Ralph resents the inference that he is losing his memory and reason, but Piggy is kindly and reassuring in support: 'You're Chief, Ralph. You remember everything' (p. 191).

The four boys walk in procession to Castle Rock, Piggy just able to glimpse the trailed butts of Sam and Eric's spears as they lead him, with Ralph at the rear. As Castle Rock comes into view Ralph rearranges the

DEATH AND DISCOVERY

order of the procession, putting himself in the lead, then Piggy followed by the twins. On the thin neck of land leading to the fort Piggy is concerned for his own safety because of his near blindness and the proximity of the cliff edge.

Ralph takes the conch and blows it. The savages appear. Roger behaves in a threatening manner; he has been left in charge while Jack is hunting. Ralph restates that he wants to call an assembly and, just as he is pressing his point about Piggy's glasses, Jack returns from a successful hunt.

Ralph charges Jack with the theft of the glasses. Indignant at the accusation, Jack stabs at Ralph who retaliates with righteous anger. The fight is halted with the boys trying to outface each other. Piggy, aware of his precarious position seated on the cliff, reminds Ralph of the reason for coming to Castle Rock. Ralph repeats the need for fire and is derogatory about the hunters' fire which is only suitable for cooking, and ineffectual as a signal.

Roger's stone throwing becomes menacing.

Piggy gains sufficient confidence from the fact that the boys are talking rather than fighting to stand up. At this point Jack orders his hunters to take the twins hostage. Ralph, incensed by this further outrage, attacks Jack. Piggy effects a lull in the violence and, through the booing of the hunters and Roger's continued stone throwing, chastens the boys for their behaviour. With the conch as his moral support, he repeatedly asks rhetorical questions about the choices they should make – 'Which is better, law and rescue, or hunting and breaking things up?' (p. 199). Whether from guilt at his questions, shame at their previous actions or recognition of Piggy as an enemy, the boys are outraged. Roger leans on the lever under the rock, tipping it down onto the approach path. Ralph sidesteps it but Piggy and the

What provokes the boys to attack Piggy?

conch are struck. The conch is shattered and Piggy is knocked off the cliff and dies on a square rock forty feet below.

Ralph is shocked but Jack, unrepentant, throws a spear which hits Ralph painfully in the chest – other spears follow. As Ralph makes his escape, Jack returns to the fort to interrogate Sam and Eric about their temerity in not joining his tribe.

COMMENT

Piggy has, quite literally, 'blind' faith in the power of the conch. It is significant that he dies at the same time that the conch – and all it symbolises – is destroyed.

Think about the parallel between the death of the pigs and of Piggy.

There is a clear and unashamed parallel between the death of the pigs and the death of Piggy. Look at Piggy's demise – 'arms and legs twitched a bit, like a pig's after it has been killed' (p. 200) – and note the similarities between that and the graphic, earlier accounts of pig killings (in Chapter 8, for example).

The focus on Piggy as 'the centre of social derision' (p. 164) – a source of amusement – ends. Previously, the humour had been caused by slapstick (falling off the 'twister' log at the assembly), pantomime mimicry (Maurice pretending to be the pig) or at the Billy Bunter-like earnestness of Piggy ('the tribe were curious to hear what amusing thing he might have to say' (p. 199)). Schoolboy humour, or indeed 'fun' of any sort, is not seen after this point.

Understandably in a novel featuring schoolboys, play – or 'Fun and games' (p. 221) – is a prominent form of behaviour. Play in Nature is often practice for something else – play fighting prepares animals for hunting, for example. In human beings it may develop beyond the need for survival into more sophisticated social skills. Roger's stone throwing, however, becomes dangerous and Jack's exaggerated dominance in the 'game' is now sinister.

Sam and Eric – Ralph's 'people' – are easily captured and converted to become members of the tribe. Observe their behaviour in the final chapter.

CHAPTER 12 – CRY OF THE HUNTERS

After escaping the hunters Ralph, bruised and bloody, reflects on his injuries and worries about whether the others are still pursuing him. He eventually comes out of hiding to spy on Castle Rock. The hunters are feasting and he decides that, for the moment at least, he is safe. He thinks about recent events and realises that Jack will not leave him in peace. He cannot fully come to terms with all that has happened. He eats some fruit and, understanding that he would not be safe in the shelter, walks on through the forest. He happens upon *What does the pig's* the remains of the pig's head; in fear and frustration he *head represent for* hits out at it and takes away the spear on which it is *Ralph?* supported.

In the thicket near Castle Rock he rests but cannot sleep for fear of what might happen. He can hear the tribe dancing and see some savages keeping lookout and regrets his isolation. Creeping towards the fort, he recognises the guards as Sam and Eric and awaits his chance to approach and speak to them.

Their manner is discouraging. They have been forced to join the tribe and they tell Ralph to go away for his own good. They also explain that Jack hates Ralph and *Sam and Eric* plans to hunt him like a pig – the boys will sweep *understand what is* across the island in line to catch him, communicating *in store for Ralph.* with wavering cries.

Ralph fears, but cannot accept, what might happen to him. Sam and Eric are unhelpful beyond telling him to go and giving him some meat. He says that he is going to hide in the thicket which, being close to the fort, may be overlooked. The twins' parting remark is that

Why does Ralph not think the boys capable of another murder?

Roger – now as terrifying as Jack – has 'sharpened a stick at both ends' (p. 210). Ralph fails to grasp the significance of this.

A little later, while tearing hungrily at the meat they had given him, Ralph hears angry voices and squeals of pain from the twins. He crawls hastily into the thicket and falls into a fitful sleep.

The hunt for Ralph begins.

He is woken in the morning by the 'cry of the hunters' and creeps further into the dense thicket. By good fortune he finds a small space – created by the tumbling rock which killed Piggy – from which he can see the fort. Soon he can hear voices. The twins have been forced to give away his position. In the silence which follows Ralph realises that one of the rocks on the cliff top is being levered to crash into the thicket. It misses him, despite the cheers of the savages at its fall.

Again there is silence; this time another massive rock thunders through the thicket, knocking him aside. Shaken but unhurt, he cowers in the undergrowth, striking out at one of the savages with his pointed stick. The unsuccessful attempts to dislodge Ralph lead the savages to try smoking him out. He heads out of the thicket towards the forest as the cries of the hunters sweep the island behind him.

Ralph realises that the signal means a hunter is unable to move forward because of the thickness of the undergrowth and considers trying to break through the cordon. He also contemplates climbing a tree. His third option is to hide and wait for them to pass. In panic his mind seizes up, unable to think clearly without Piggy's help.

At last he decides to find somewhere to hide. Running past the pig's remains, he is aware that the forest is now on fire. He seeks out a dense, sunless thicket to hide in as the raging fire burns the fruit trees. As Ralph

considers his fate, he spots a savage approaching with a
stick 'sharpened at both ends' (p. 219). It is identical to
his own and he understands its significance at last.

*Ralph gathers
strength from his
memories of Piggy
and Simon.*

He remains in place (Simon's statement that he would
get back home reassuring him) until the tension is too
great. Finally he breaks out and, dodging the spears,
heads for the beach. He runs, almost numb and light-
headed with terror and exhaustion, until he stumbles
and falls on the sand.

*Contrast Jack now
with the way he
looks and behaves
in the early part of
the novel.*

Raising himself in expectation of the onslaught of the
savages, he is faced by a naval officer, who has seen the
smoke. He is alarmed by the boy's unkempt appearance
and shocked that two boys have been killed on the
island. As others emerge – including Jack – the officer
expresses his surprise that British boys were not better
able to survive. Ralph and other boys break down in
relief at the end of their ordeal.

COMMENT

After killing Piggy, Roger has become sadistic. In
sharpening the stick at both ends – like the one used to
impale the pig's head – he is obviously preparing to kill,
and presumably behead, Ralph. As Sam and Eric
pronounce, 'He's a terror' (p. 209).

Does the ending live up to your expectations?

Ralph has become an outcast, partly because he 'had some sense' (p. 205). He is alone now that Piggy and Simon are dead and Sam and Eric have been forced to change sides. Ralph's isolation, fear and pain are all described graphically. The atmosphere is tense and heightened by degrees to a climax. Do you think the ending is a disappointing let-down or a fitting resolution of the tension that has built up?

The naval officer says that British boys should have put up a 'better show' (p. 222) and, he implies, not end up like savages. This is a romanticised (see Literary terms) view of their experience, as if they were characters from an adventure story like *The Coral Island*. The officer's enthusiasm echoes that of the boys in the first chapter and, in one sense, brings the story full circle. Yet, despite this, we are left with a lingering feeling of the darker realities of human nature.

The picture of Jack as a little boy belies the truth of his primitive, underlying aggression and savagery.

Ralph's reaction at the end of the book is as much grief as relief. 'Ralph wept for the end of innocence, the darkness of man's heart, and the fall through the air of the true, wise friend called Piggy' (p. 223).

GLOSSARY   **pax** (*Latin*) peace; old-fashioned public school expression, used to declare the end of an argument
They're going to do you they're going to punish or kill you
Jolly good show good effort, well done

TEST YOURSELF (Chapters 9–12)

A

Identify the speaker.

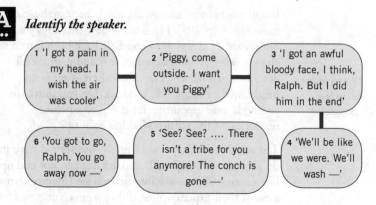

1 'I got a pain in my head. I wish the air was cooler'

2 'Piggy, come outside. I want you Piggy'

3 'I got an awful bloody face, I think, Ralph. But I did him in the end'

6 'You got to go, Ralph. You go away now —'

5 'See? See? …. There isn't a tribe for you anymore! The conch is gone —'

4 'We'll be like we were. We'll wash —'

Identify the person(s) to whom this comment refers.

7 'He's going to beat Wilfred'

8 Still he did not move but lay there, his face sideways on the earth, his eyes looking dully before him

9 He forgot his wounds, his hunger and thirst and became fear; hopeless fear on flying feet

Check your answers on page 86.

B

Consider these issues.

a Why Simon persists in climbing the mountain when he is so weak.

b The author's development of drama and tension.

c Character traits are fully realised – often to sinister effect – in this section.

d What techniques the author uses to help you sympathise with Ralph.

e The information, both useful and frightening, that the twins give Ralph.

f How the naval officer might relate his experience and findings to another person.

g Your own feelings about the finale of the novel.

h What ideas, thoughts and lessons you are left with after reading *Lord of the Flies*.

y

PART THREE

COMMENTARY

THEMES

Taken at face value, *Lord of the Flies* is a simple tale. Golding himself regarded it as a modern fable (see Literary Terms) which can be enjoyed on more complex levels. One way to appreciate this is by exploring some of the themes of the book, to throw light on what William Golding wanted to say and on the times he was writing in. We discuss five themes below, but don't let this stop you finding and thinking about others of your own.

GOOD AND EVIL

The battle between good and evil is a central theme of *Lord of the Flies*. It appears in many conflicts – between the conch group and the savages, between the boys and the terrifying 'beast' and between rescue from a passing ship and imprisonment on the increasingly insane island, to name but a few.

Early in the novel, good is in the ascendancy. The conch provides a symbol (see Literary Terms) of the decency and order of the society that the boys have come from (see Law and order below). Ralph organises the construction of shelters – mostly, in fact, the selfless work of him and Simon – and a fire to signal to ships with. The boys spend the majority of their time playing and there are a few accidents, such as the fire that kills the birthmarked boy, but with Ralph's benign government, good is always dominant.

This situation is threatened as Jack continues his attempts to take over the conch group. He fails in this – a small victory for good – and sulks off to form his own 'tribe'. From then on, evil takes control. Boys join Jack's tribe because he hunts pigs and doesn't make them

work. Ralph, representing the forces of good, is
paralysed by indecision and has no effective response.
Jack's tribe grows and his malevolence with it. Piggy's
glasses are violently stolen, leaving him sightless. When
the remainder of the conch group goes to retrieve the
spectacles, Sam and Eric are captured and Piggy slain.
Only the naval officer's intervention prevents the
complete triumph of evil over good.

Golding is giving us a warning about the power of evil,
that if the good in people is not fostered then evil will
take its place. The human urge to destroy will be
unleashed and in the modern age there seem to be no
limits to the harm this can do (see Cold War paranoia
below). In this sense, *Lord of the Flies* can be seen as a
cautionary tale, advocating change before it is too late.

LAW AND ORDER

The boys have come from a society in which orderliness
is the norm and they attempt to continue this when
they first arrive on the island.

Very quickly, the conch comes to symbolise (see Literary
Terms and Symbolism in Language & Style) the values
of this previous existence. The boys cannot talk at
meetings unless they are holding the conch, and are thus
forced to treat whoever is speaking with respect. This
means that Piggy – in many ways a natural victim – is
able to air intelligent thoughts that lead to
improvements in the boys' lives. So toilets are moved
away from the shelters and the boys try to keep a fire
burning at all times. 'Parliaments' of this kind have
always been key elements of successful civilisations, from
Viking *tings* to our own system of government.

The other symbol associated with Piggy, his glasses,
exposes a different side of law and order on the island.
Rightfully they belong to Piggy, who needs them to see

properly. Used with his permission, they also start the fires that are essential both to rescue and hygienically-cooked food. Jack – at school a figure of authority and order as head of the choir – refuses to respect Piggy's right to the glasses, first punching him and breaking a lens, then stealing the pair to start fires. In doing so, he challenges the law and order that has kept life on the island reasonable under Ralph. When the boys no longer accept law and order after this, Ralph is powerless and darker, more evil forces take over (see Good and evil above).

DISCIPLINE

William Golding was a teacher at Bishop Wordsworth's School for nine years before he wrote *Lord of the Flies*. In this time he grew unhappy with the English public school tradition that firm discipline was the best means of turning children into young adults.

The island is like a laboratory in which Golding can analyse the tensions that exist within a school. By removing the adults, he sets free the impulses and desires of the schoolboys and – almost – allows them to run their full course. So Jack, who we presume to be arrogant and bullying at school, becomes first a wrecker of Ralph and Piggy's sensible plans, then a dictator and finally a murderer. Piggy, on the other hand, is a permanent victim of Jack's bullying and is killed. Clearly these disasters could have been prevented by the normal orderliness of school life (see Law and order above).

Golding goes on to explore some of the problems that harsh discipline can conceal. A vivid demonstration is provided by the boys' sex lives. At first glance, sex is avoided in the book, not even getting the vague mentions that toiletry functions do. Looking closer, we find consistently sexual language used to describe the pig hunts and their re-enactments. For instance, 'Ralph too was fighting to get near, to get a handful of that brown, vulnerable flesh' (p. 126). This comes to a head later in a hunt which almost reads like a gang rape, ending as the 'sow collapsed under them and they were heavy and fulfilled upon her' (p. 149). Sex is taboo at school and continues the same on the island. So the boys' sexual urges come out in other ways, in particular in a desire to hurt the defenceless pigs. In the real world many serial killers and rapists share this inability to find sexual satisfaction in conventional and socially acceptable ways, and we see the results in the news every day.

Is Golding despairing of the school system he taught in? Not necessarily, for (as we saw in Law and order) Piggy's brains and Ralph's self-discipline result in positive achievements early in the novel, such as the fire and the shelters. And school discipline would restrict Jack's worst excesses. Difficulties only arise when this communal discipline is overwhelmed by the arbitrary discipline of a cruel leader – Jack – or immersed in the frenzy of a mob (see Crowd mentality below). What is needed is a balance between firm discipline and a certain creative freedom, and it is the absence of this that Golding is criticising in the schools of the time.

CROWD MENTALITY

At the start of the novel, we find a natural group already formed when Jack appears at the head of the choir. This group is disciplined, a fact which is of great help in hunting pigs, when good organisation is of paramount importance.

As order on the island breaks down (see Law and order above), the boys begin to behave differently when in groups. Pig hunts become ritualised and frenzied, marked by the chant, 'Kill the pig! Cut his throat! Kill the pig! Bash him in!' The boys act as a mob at these times and start to lose their individual identities. This absolves them of any direct blame for what happens and distracts them from their plight on the island.

The climax of this crowd mentality comes when Simon returns with news that the 'beast' is actually a dead pilot. He stumbles into the midst of the near-hysterical savages during a night-time thunderstorm, and is himself taken to be the 'beast'. The mob, including Ralph, 'leapt on to the beast, screamed, struck, bit, tore. There were no words, and no movements but the tearing of teeth and claws' (p. 168). Afterwards Piggy and Ralph have great difficulty accepting that they have murdered Simon: '"It was an accident," said Piggy suddenly, "that's what it was. An accident."' (p. 173).

In a mob, everyday life loses its meaning. Individuals are swallowed up and the mob seeks out those who are weak or simply outsiders to vent its fury on. There have been pogroms – where mobs kill members of minority groups – throughout European history, with Jews by far the most frequent victims. We see from recent events in Bosnia and Croatia that this is not a thing of the past.

Foremost in Golding's mind, however, when describing mob behaviour was Nazi Germany. Jack in many ways echoes Hitler. At first charismatic and seeming to offer easy solutions to difficult situations, both learnt to use the fury of the mob against their enemies. Hitler turned mobs against Communists, Jews, homosexuals and, indeed, many of his own followers to eliminate opponents and terrify everyone else. Jack likewise kills and intimidates until complete control is almost in his hands. Witness particularly Eric's orders to hunt Ralph and throw his spear 'like at a pig' (p. 208). Jack wants to use the pig-hunting mob frenzy to kill Ralph.

COLD WAR PARANOIA

The first use of atomic weapons in war – at Hiroshima in Japan on 6 August 1945 – undermined many people's assumptions about life. Suddenly it seemed possible for the whole of civilisation to be destroyed by a single conflict.

This was not a practical problem until 1949, when the Soviet Union exploded its first A-bomb and the Cold War began in earnest. This was never an open war, although numerous conflicts, such as Korea, Vietnam and Afghanistan, were fought in its name. Rather it was an ideological battle in which anyone suspected of being the enemy would be attacked. Through the late forties and early fifties the infamous McCarthy 'witch-hunts' were conducted in America. Many respected and influential people were destroyed by – often false – accusations that they were Communists. This paranoia – imagining that good, patriotic citizens were traitors – is deeply reminiscent of Jack and of Hitler's Germany (see Crowd mentality above).

In this context Golding wrote *Lord of the Flies*. A great deal of its stark confrontation – Jack against Ralph, savages against the conch group, even evil against good (see above) – stems from the Cold War outlook. More specifically, the boys have been stranded by the Cold War turning into a real war. Their plane has presumably been shot down and the 'beast' is a pilot who has ejected from his warplane.

On top of this, Golding was impressed by the Existentialist philosophy of writers such as Albert Camus, Jean-Paul Sartre and Samuel Beckett. Put simply, Existentialism claimed that God did not exist and that individuals were solely responsible for their own actions. So if you kill someone – as the savage mob does Simon – you must accept that you are responsible for your part of it, with no excuses. Ralph, as the force for good, tries to do this after Simon's death – 'That was murder' (p. 172) – but even he fails.

Golding seems to be making several related points. Firstly he is saying that the world we know can be destroyed by atomic weapons. The island itself can be seen as a metaphor (see Literary Terms) for the earth after a nuclear holocaust. Secondly, he is showing that the response to the Cold War – an hysterical and irrational desire to be on one side or the other, savage or conch – can only bring this nuclear disaster closer. Finally, he provides a way forward, through individuals taking responsibility for themselves and not being manipulated by the mob mentality. If this had happened on the island, Piggy and Simon would both be alive when the naval officer arrives, and Ralph would probably still be chief, exercising his influence for good.

Instead society on the island breaks down, and we do have the deaths of Simon and Piggy. Golding is warning that a continuation of the Cold War, without a substantial increase in personal responsibility, will lead to the fate of the boys on the island for all humanity.

STRUCTURE

A simple story *Lord of the Flies* follows standard novel form with a simple and direct storyline. Although it is rightly regarded as a great piece of twentieth century literature by many people, it would be fair to say that it is limited – and deliberately so – in several obvious ways. For instance, the structure is dictated (as in any novel) by the characters and setting; Golding places his characters on an island, hence the events are largely a product of those people, their reactions and relationships as they engage with each other and that environment. Apart from the naval officer and ratings at the end and the parachutist halfway through, no one arrives on the island but the boys. And no one leaves – with the exception of the three who die, departing in a spiritual sense.

The boys then, are placed in a vacuum; the story is moved along and structured by their social chemistry as it evolves in that restricted setting. That this works in so powerful and convincing a way, with such limiting and unlikely ingredients, seems a surprise. But, as Novalis – the German Romantic poet – suggested, 'Character is Fate'. The use of child-characters, too, would appear unpromising, but the rivalry between Jack and Ralph – the result of their conflicting natures – together with their supporting cohorts, and Simon's subplot (see Literary Terms), carries the story – but only in part.

Although no other living character visits the island during the boys' stay, the descent of the parachutist injects an important element into the structure of the action. The 'beast', in whatever shape – dead pilot, the 'fear' or as Simon, mistakenly killed in its place – provides another source of tension.

These two strands of human conflict on one side and fear of the beast on the other grow as the story develops. This expansion is coupled with the gradual and simultaneous degeneration of morals and morale towards an inevitable – and perhaps anticipated – climax.

It is also worthwhile to consider the structure of the novel in terms of time and space, and as three distinct 'blocks' of action and development. All the events take place over a period of several weeks. How many is uncertain, but the passage of time is suggested by the loss of memory in one boy and Ralph's observation about the growth of the boys' hair. The first four chapters establish the characters and their behaviour; the middle section looks at the development of differences, exploring fears and obsessions; and the last four show the solution of those conflicts with death and finally, deliverance.

CHARACTERS

RALPH

Ralph is portrayed as the epitome of British boyhood – handsome, sporting, decent and honourable, but not possessed of any great intelligence or imagination. He is kindly – notice how, after Jack is defeated in the first election and Simon has just recovered from his faint, he chooses them to go exploring with him. Golding describes him as mild-featured: 'there was a mildness about his mouth and eyes that proclaimed no devil' (p. 11). He has no hidden depth or unhealthy character traits.

Ralph's father is a commander in the Royal Navy and he has travelled fairly widely. His wish to return to the oft-described image of his middle-class home sustains him through his ordeal. His views on cleanliness are not typical for boys of his age! Again this is linked to his natural sense of decency. His disgust at the state of the

Practical and
determined
Fair-minded
Athletic
Comfortable and
middle-class
Kind
Has common sense
Good-looking
Quite confident

boys is largely due to a comparison with what he sees as acceptable levels of hygiene and civilised behaviour.

Having a father in the Armed Forces may go some way to promoting a sense of order (see Law and Order in Themes) and appreciation for reasoned argument and systematic problem-solving. Ralph, after all, devises the convention that only the boy holding the conch is allowed to speak.

He possesses the confidence of his class, but little of its arrogance. Although he behaves with boyish superiority over Piggy when the boys arrive – even using his knowledge of the fat boy's nickname to raise a laugh – he lacks the malice of Jack. Despite recognising Piggy as an outsider he develops both respect and affection for him and his qualities.

Ralph exhibits a quiet authority which the boys appreciate and prefer to Jack's more strident and threatening manner. Ralph's leadership style and skills of oratory improve with experience. These, together with a perseverance on practical matters and confidence in his own ideology, lend weight to his suitability as chief.

However, it is not until he learns the ability to think more deeply and incisively that he is able to function effectively. Piggy's bequest, the ability to think (when pursued by the hunters) is ultimately responsible for his survival.

y

PIGGY

Intelligent
Asthmatic
Father dead
Mother – fate
unknown
Has worn glasses
since he was three
Overweight
Lives with aunt in
a sweet shop
Speaks
ungrammatically

Piggy's unprepossessing appearance and isolation prevent him from making a full contribution to life on the island. Even Ralph is dismissive of him at first, regarding him, perhaps correctly, as a whining and overweight hypochondriac who can be ordered about. Piggy is the boy who would be chosen last for the football team. He seems to have little to commend him when survival on a desert island is at stake.

He is set apart in other ways too. His background is plainly working class, not middle class like Ralph, Jack and the choir. Presumably he is a scholarship boy. As Ralph observes, 'Piggy was an outsider, not only by accent, which did not matter, but by fat, and ass-mar, and specs, and a certain disinclination for manual labour' (p. 70). He is socially unacceptable and somewhat inept. He fears people, possibly because of his experience of past treatment and cruelty.

Yet, for all this, he is probably the most intelligent boy on the island. He has the foresight and good sense of an older person; he exhibits a degree of caution and some organising ability. He displays moral and physical courage in upholding the supremacy of the conch but most important of all – he is a thinker.

It is his ability to think which he passes to Ralph. When Jack says Piggy and Ralph are alike he means in the sense that they are thoughtful and serious-minded, rather than in any physical way. Piggy is not only imaginative but can solve problems using lateral and/or rational thought. Even if his courage fails him in practice, he is logical in his treatment of the theory. He is protective of his rights and, like Ralph, fair-minded and egalitarian.

His intelligence is the natural complement to Ralph's common sense. Their relationship is symbiotic – each supports the other – like Don Quixote and Sancho Panza in Cervantes's famous novel, or, more appropriately, Robinson Crusoe and Man Friday. They are more influential and effective when working together, each possessing qualities that the other lacks.

JACK MERRIDEW

Head boy, leader of the choir

Red hair

Aggressive and dominant

Arrogant

Pugnacious

Envious

Dictatorial

Chief of the savages

Hunter

Jack is a character Golding has clearly intended you dislike. He provides little basis for empathy in either his words or his actions. Even from his dramatic entrance – the procession of capped and gowned choirboys along the beach, in itself anachronistic and sinister – he is arrogant and aggravating. He assumes leadership on the basis that he is chapter chorister, can sing C sharp and is head boy. None of which necessarily fit him for high office on a desert island, except possibly the last. Being head boy only means that he is familiar with the task of leadership, not that he is automatically skilled at it. In many respects the opposite is true, as we discover.

His main contribution to the survival of the boys is to track the pigs and provide meat. Meat is not absolutely essential to their survival (the island has fruit, crabs and shellfish as well) yet he insists on its importance. In this sense he represents Man the Hunter; although he sees the whole experience on the island as a game, he exhibits a basic, primeval instinct – the urge to hunt.

Unfortunately, his simplistic and single-minded approach is self-destructive and lacking in foresight. Two examples illustrate this: the boys kill a sow, which could have bred and provided future meat and, in their hunt for Ralph, they destroy the fruit trees. These two, rather precipitate, actions mean that they would eventually have starved.

The other consequence of Jack's hunting instinct is bizarre and sinister. He goes from hunting animals to hunting people. Survival then becomes not a matter of finding food but manifests itself in warfare. He uses the weapons and skills developed from necessity to enforce his will (see Crowd mentality in Themes).

Although Jack's personality traits make him what he is, background and conditioning, it could be argued, are also contributory factors. On the one hand he has the archetypal, red-haired temper, together with a natural dominance. On the other, his training in a very middle class, religious and ritualistic school environment is reflected in the behaviour and actions of his tribe. They wear strange garments, sing and chant and administer seemingly arbitrary punishments.

Jack's physical appearance throughout the novel is also a deliberate and blatant warning sign. His red hair stands out, as well as being associated with a fiery temper it also, significantly, indicates danger. When he, quite literally, masks his appearance with paint, far from neutralising his venom and pugnacity it gives it free rein. Hidden behind it he can absolve himself of decency and responsibility, realising his most extreme and evil potential (see Good and evil in Themes).

Jack's lack of humility, along with his bravado, selfish and dictatorial leadership are all intended to conflict with the ideals Golding creates in some of his other characters. Jack's final appearance in Chapter 12 portrays him as a little boy, perhaps re-emphasising how thin the veneer of conditioning and respectability can be when set against the primal instincts shown in his earlier actions.

SIMON

Simon exhibits a number of contradictory characteristics. He is helpful and community-spirited – helping with the shelters – yet is, on occasions, reclusive and solitary. He is, as Ralph says, 'always about' (p. 59) but spends time alone in the forest. Although he is shy and timid during the assemblies – not being able to bring himself to speak his deepest thoughts honestly – he shows great courage in other respects; he walks alone through the jungle at night and even climbs the mountain to face the beast.

Shy
Kind and
thoughtful
Sensitive
Courageous
Strange
Introvert
Intelligent and
perceptive
'Spiritual'

He is described on numerous occasions as 'batty', 'queer', 'funny' and 'crackers', but quite what form this strangeness takes is never really explicit. The boys lack the vocabulary to define and so pigeon-hole him as a particular type. He is evidently kind and considerate to others – helping the littluns and showing concern for Piggy. He is thought of as odd principally because he is different.

None of the other boys, with perhaps the exception of Piggy, have anything like his insight. It is Simon who tries to explain the notion of evil which manifests itself in 'the fear' and 'the beast', by asking, 'What's the dirtiest thing there is?' (p. 97). He has the intellect and maturity to understand the concept, but lacks the language to express it. We can only assume that his perception has been regarded as strange and alien on other occasions – in part accounting for his strangeness – which is why he is reluctant to voice his feelings with confidence.

Despite saying comparatively little in the book, it is often Simon who captures moments of potential enlightenment in a single sentence. He assures Ralph, for example, that he will get back home and puts into words Ralph's wonderment at the immensity of the sea. It is Simon who feels the need to go up the mountain to see the beast for what it is but his insistence is, once again, ignored. He shows determination in discovering the truth for himself, but is killed by the boys before he can share his knowledge with them.

He has considerable strength of mind but is frail of body, and enters the story fainting, something he appears to do regularly. He seems to suffer from epilepsy or some similar condition. Simon is often regarded as a prophet – even a saint or Christ figure – and there are certainly images to support such a view. His perception and individuality, combined with his human vulnerability make him an intriguing character however you see him.

ROGER

Sadistic
Jack's lieutenant

The degeneration from man to animal, from red-cheeked choirboy to premeditated killer, can be seen most obviously in Roger. He is Jack's lieutenant, and it is significant that it is to Roger that Jack shows the clay which they later use for their masks. Roger is Jack's partner in crime but ultimately outstrips even him in barbarism. He has, from the start, a sadistic streak, teasing Henry in the stone throwing incident and, by the end, his stone throwing leads to Piggy's death. It is Roger who sharpens the spear 'at both ends' (p. 210) in preparation for the hunting of Ralph; its use is clear and horrifying to us, although Ralph finds it difficult to comprehend

SAM AND ERIC

The twins

Act as one person

Interestingly, Sam and Eric do not join Jack's tribe at first and only finally do so when forced. Perhaps, behaving as one person they are strong enough or sufficiently secure in themselves not to be influenced by Jack. Whatever the reason, they become, and remain for much of the novel, Ralph's 'tribe'. They are treated as one person, even when taking a shift at the fire. Like many twins they have their own understanding of a private language and finish each other's sentences.

It is not until the night of the raid that they disagree and fight with each other in their sleep. When Sam says that he got 'mixed up with myself' (p. 185) does he mean that he literally got tangled up or is he fighting with his other self – his twin? This might be interpreted as depicting a human being in a dilemma, good and evil fighting within him (see Good and evil in Themes).

MINOR CHARACTERS

MAURICE   In much the same way that Roger is next in command to Jack, Maurice is Roger's henchman. However, whereas Roger goes on to become 'a terror' (p. 209), Maurice retains much of his original sense of sin and a natural reserve. After the incident on the beach with the 'littluns', he feels guilty in a way that Roger does not. Throughout the novel Maurice, although a loyal savage, remains stolid and unimaginative.

ROBERT   Robert is further down the pecking order of the savages than Maurice but, unlike him, is a natural 'follower'. He fits comfortably into their life and activities. It is Robert, together with Maurice, who skewers the pig's head on a stick and enters into the pantomime version of pig killing which is the precursor of the event which leads to Simon's death.

PERCIVAL WEMYS MADISON

Percival's name is supposed to indicate a very middle class background. Even early on his conditioned response begins to dwindle, 'Percival Wemys Madison, The Vicarage, Harcourt St. Anthony, Hants, telephone, telephone, tele—' (p. 94). By the end of the novel, 'Percival Wemys Madison sought in his head for an incantation that had faded clean away' (p. 222). The influences of his home life and background are made to look thin and superficial alongside the starker reality of his experiences on the island.

THE BOY WITH THE BIRTHMARK

Throughout the novel the 'littluns' remain largely anonymous; Golding deliberately gives this little boy a physical characteristic which makes him memorable. Hence, when he is missing after the over-zealous fire lighting on the mountain, it is obvious that he has disappeared and the boys are made strongly aware of the consequences of their actions.

THE PARACHUTIST

Having asked for a sign from the outside world, the dead airman is not, perhaps, what the boys had in mind. It is interesting that none of them see him for what he is – a dead human being – but rather as a representation of defeat, death and decay. He is also the manifestation of evil and the boys' worst fears in the form of 'the beast'. Only Simon gets close to recognising the reality and facts of the matter, treating him with dignity and compassion.

THE NAVAL OFFICER

In contrast with the dead airman, the naval officer offers a sanitised view of the war and Service life. In his white, Tropical kit he appears like a knight in shining armour; the cavalry – a final cliché – offering the boys deliverance. He is clearly shocked that British boys could not put up a 'better show' (p. 222) when he is told about the deaths and possesses a rather romantic notion of what life must have been like for them. His arrival echoes Ralph's idea that his father, 'a commander in the Navy' (p. 14), would eventually rescue them. There is irony (see Literary Terms) in the fact that they are being returned to the same war which caused the demise of the parachutist – a 'war' no less brutal that which afflicted all the boys on the island.

LANGUAGE & STYLE

When a writer has conceived a plot, developed characters, considered themes and related issues – all that is contained in the initial creative process – only then can the craft begin. Because his or her medium is the written word and the intention to communicate to an unseen reader in a common language, on the basis of little shared experience or identity, linguistic choices are, to say the least, difficult! A bewildering array of devices, a clutter of vocabulary and an armoury of figures of speech are at the author's disposal. Although writers use these deliberately to create effect, they can use them with an ease and precision that does not appear contrived or clumsy. It is this that shows the writer's craft, and this which we, as teachers and students, point to and admire.

A modern fable

Golding intended to convey a number of messages in his 'modern fable' (see Literary Terms), none of which were light-hearted or flippant. His pessimism about the natural state of human beings, their culpability and sinfulness and his own cynicism about life inevitably inform the style and tone of his writing. None of this is trivial; his tone is one of hopelessness and despondency at the inevitability of evil and unpleasant things happening. Yet he does not overstate the more morbid perspective, nor does he become maudlin. He shows us plainly what the consequences might be, then leaves us to think and to learn.

What Golding has to teach us is delivered objectively, without apparent bias. In passages of description, we are told what is happening with the faithfulness of a neutral observer; indeed, we must search hard sometimes for meanings. In sections of dialogue, exchanges are pithy and direct but the nuances of speech and action are related without prejudice, so we may draw our own conclusions.

Golding used a wide range of literary devices.

Scrutiny of some of the descriptive prose passages reveals that Golding used a wide range of literary 'devices' and figures of speech. Pages 60-63 are a rewarding point at which to start looking for this. *Lord of the Flies* contains examples of allegory (see Literary Terms); similes and metaphors abound, together with hypallage, irony, slang, symbolism and imagery.

Irony

Golding's use of irony is both interesting and highly relevant to the tone and message of the novel. In terms of style, irony provides a powerful vehicle for some, often quite macabre, statements about life and fate. Irony is somewhat easier to illustrate than define; the following points may help you understand it.

- Piggy is angry about the forest fire and the disappearance of the boy with the birthmark – but Piggy's glasses were used to start the fire, so he is indirectly responsible.
- Simon returns to the camp with the truth about the 'beast', which could dispel the boys' fears. He is killed before he can tell his news.
- After the raid, Ralph and Eric feel proud of how well they fought. They were, in fact, fighting each other in the darkness.
- The rock which kills Piggy clears a space in the thicket – enabling Ralph to escape the hunters and so survive.

- Jack's hunters set fire to the bushes to smoke out and kill Ralph. It is this fire which draws attention to the island and effects the boys' rescue.
- The boys are taken away from the 'war' on the island by a naval officer who is involved in, and returning them to, another war.

It can be seen then that irony is a type of reversal of ideas, and shows how seemingly good events often lead to bad – and vice versa.

Dialogue

Why does Golding write such terse dialogue?

In contrast with the complexity of the descriptive pieces, the sections of dialogue are terse and almost monosyllabic. The best way for you to see this is by studying some short sections in detail yourself. The boys rarely speak more than a few sentences at a time; often their utterances amount to just a few words and their vocabulary – for boys who are quite well educated – is limited. (Try counting the number of words, syllables and sentences in a typical section of speech in any chapter.) They also resort to boyish slang and mild swearing; their exclamations mirror those of cartoon or comic characters and they lack some of the vocabulary needed to discuss more sophisticated concepts.

Symbolism

Lord of the Flies can be viewed as like an onion – it has a simple storyline with ever increasing 'rings' of meaning around that central core. As a fable (see Literary Terms) it is uncomplicated, but the surrounding 'rings' cover many deeper issues. The story contains, for instance, a number of symbolic (see Literary Terms) objects. The conch is more than just a shell, useful for attracting attention and summoning the boys to meetings. It is like a church bell calling the faithful and embodies some of the ritual of religious ceremonies. For the boys on the island it also imposes a sense of order (see Law and order in Themes). Only one person can hold the conch, so only one person can speak at a time and, unlike Jack's assemblies, everyone is given that right. The conch can, therefore, symbolise free speech, democracy, order and unity.

Piggy's glasses are more than an aid to his poor eyesight. To the boys the glasses symbolise fire without which, as Ralph repeatedly proclaims, they cannot be rescued or cook the meat which Jack provides. Fire then is representative of life, but sadly and ironically (see Literary Terms), it is also the element which causes the death of the boy with the birthmark and very nearly leads Ralph to the same fate. By association, the glasses symbolise life – and death – knowledge, power and dominance.

Does the Lord of the Flies – *the pig's head – symbolise the 'beast' or something more complex?*

The beast, whether real or imaginary, is symbolic. It represents what Ralph calls 'the darkness of man's heart' (p. 223). This is the 'beast' present in each of us – the capacity for evil and wrongdoing (see Good and evil in Themes). This beast must be served and accommodated and so the Lord of the Flies (the pig's head on a stick) becomes its shrine. The boys' recognition of evil, or the Devil, is embodied in the sacrifice they make after each kill.

The pig's head symbolises all of this to Simon, and also the cynicism of adults and the hollowness and superficiality of their world. It is Simon who sees the parachutist as epitomising the capacity of adults for death and destruction. He symbolically frees this 'unknown soldier' when he releases the suspension lines of the parachute.

Although symbolism is, in part, tied to objects, it can be seen here that actions can also be symbolic. Think, for example, of the hunters baptising themselves with the blood of the pig, or the death of the sow representing the boys relinquishing a mother figure – and so, parental ties and innocence.

Imagery

Images (see Literary Terms) are 'pictures' which reflect (and so symbolise) something else. These pictures can be in the form of simple similes and metaphors (see Literary Terms) which allow us to better imagine an incident or scene by drawing on our own experience. For example, think about expressions such as 'like raindrops on a wire' or 'like an angry eye' (p. 63). Or consider the metaphorical use of language: 'a bowl of heat and light' (p. 61) and 'darkness poured out' (p.62). Beyond these are more complex pictures which demand more involved parallels to be drawn.

Most readers will be able to empathise with images like light and dark, hot and cold or clear and opaque. The contrasts of positive and negative, (and therefore good and bad) are obvious and unashamed.

Make a list of the images associated with the main characters.

Images are often themed in the novel. Simon is linked to natural images and images of death are often encountered where Jack is present. Ralph contemplates the sea, another natural image. Simon is prophet-like in many ways, including his withdrawal to the jungle to meditate. He is seen being 'tempted' by the Lord of the Flies; haloed in light when he dies; bringing a 'truth' which nobody listens to; freeing the dead airman from, quite literal, corruption and expressing spiritual understanding. Other images are rewarding if we take particular notice of Simon in this context.

PART FOUR

STUDY SKILLS

HOW TO USE QUOTATIONS

One of the secrets of success in writing essays is the way you use quotations. There are five basic principles:

- Put inverted commas at the beginning and end of the quotation
- Write the quotation exactly as it appears in the orginal
- Do not use a quotation that repeats what you have just written
- Use the quotation so that it fits into your sentence
- Keep the quotation as short as possible

Quotations should be used to develop the line of thought in your essays. Your comment should not duplicate what is in your quotation. For example:

Jack thinks he should be chief automatically because he is head boy, 'I'm chapter chorister and head boy. I can sing C sharp'.

Far more effective is to write:

Jack thinks he should be chief automatically because he is, 'chapter chorister and head boy'.

However, the most sophisticated way of using the writer's words is to embed them into your sentence:

Ralph thought that Simon was fun-loving because his eyes were 'delightfully gay and wicked', which was partly true.

When you use quotations in this way, you are demonstating the ability to use text as evidence to support your ideas – not simply including words from the original to prove you have read it.

Everyone writes differently. Work through the suggestions given here and adapt the advice to suit your own style and interests. This will improve your essay-writing skills and allow your personal voice to emerge.

The following points indicate in ascending order the skills of essay writing:

- Picking out one or two facts about the story and adding the odd detail
- Writing about the text by retelling the story
- Retelling the story and adding a quotation here and there
- Organising an answer which explains what is happening in the text and giving quotations to support what you write

....

- Writing in such a way as to show that you have thought about the intentions of the writer of the text and that you understand the techniques used
- Writing at some length, giving you viewpoint on the text and commenting by picking out details to support your views
- Looking at the text as a work of art, demonstrating clear critical judgement and explaining to the reader of your essay how the enjoyment of the text is assisted by literary devices, linguistic effects and psychological insights; showing how the text relates to the time when it was written

The dotted line above represents the division between lower and higher level grades. Higher level performance begins when you start to consider your response as a reader of the text. The highest level is reached when you offer an enthusiastic personal response and show how this piece of literature is a product of its time.

Coursework Set aside an hour or so at the start of your work to plan
essay what you have to do.

- List all the points you feel are needed to cover the
  task. Collect page references of information and
  quotations that will support what you have to say. A
  helpful tool is the highlighter pen: this saves
  painstaking copying and enables you to target
  precisely what you want to use.
- Focus on what you consider to be the main points of
  the essay. Try to sum up your argument in a single
  sentence, which could be the closing sentence of your
  essay. Depending on the essay title, it could be a
  statement about a character: Ralph is the character
  Golding intended his readers to admire most, but he
  could have survived better if Piggy had lived; an
  opinion about setting: Golding chose the island to
  show that 'no man is an island entire of himself' –
  human beings need other people, social order and a
  breadth of experience to survive. They cannot do so
  alone; or a judgement on a theme: The main theme
  appears to be that all human beings possess a sense of
  evil, to some degree.
- Make a short essay plan. Use the first paragraph to
  introduce the argument you wish to make. In the
  following paragraphs develop this argument with
  details, examples and other possible points of view.
  Sum up your argument in the last paragraph. Check
  you have answered the question.
- Write the essay, remembering all the time the central
  point you are making.
- On completion, go back over what you have written
  to eliminate careless errors and improve expression.
  Read it aloud to yourself, or, if you are feeling more
  confident, to relative or friend.

If you can, try to type you essay, using a word processor.
This will allow you to correct and improve your writing
without spoiling its appearance.

Examination essay

The essay written in an examination often carries more marks than the coursework essay even though it is written under considerable time pressure.

In the revision period build up notes on various aspects of the text you are using. Fortunately, in acquiring this set of York Notes on *Lord of the Flies*, you have made a prudent beginning! York Notes are set out to give you vital information and help you to construct your personal overview of the text.

Make notes with appropriate quotations about the key issues of the set text. Go into the examination knowing your text and having a clear set of opinions about it.

In the examination

In most English Literature examinations, you can take in copies of your set books. This is an enormous advantage although it may lull you into a false sense of security. Beware! There is simply not enough time in an examination to read the book from scratch.

- Read the question paper carefully and remind yourself what you have to do.
- Look at the questions on your set texts to select the one that most interests you and mentally work out the points you wish to stress.
- Remind yourself of the time available and how you are going to use it.
- Briefly map out a short plan in note form that will keep your writing on track and illustrate the key argument you want to make.
- Then set about writing it.
- When you have finished, check through to eliminate errors.

To summarise,
these are the
keys to success:

- Know the text
- Have a clear understanding of and opinions on the storyline, characters, setting, themes and writer's concerns
- Select the right material
- Plan and write a clear response, continually bearing the question in mind

SAMPLE ESSAY PLAN

A typical essay question on *Lord of the Flies* is followed by a sample essay plan in note form. This does not present the only answer to the question, merely one answer. Do not be afraid to include your own ideas, and leave out some of those in the sample! Remember that quotations are essential to prove and illustrate the points you make.

Show how the sense of order on the island deteriorates over the course of the novel.

Introduction

- William Golding wanted to explore the fragility of our civilisation. So, in *Lord of the Flies*, he abandons a group of schoolboys on a desert island and chronicles the battle between order and chaos that follows.

Part 1

The establishment of order

- Ralph uses the conch to assemble the boys in one place
- Jack, the head boy, feels he should be chief. When a democratic vote is held, however, Ralph wins comfortably
- The conch becomes a symbol of the order of the world the boys have come from. To speak at a meeting one must hold the conch
- Ralph points out that a fire is essential for signalling to ships, and so being rescued. A great fire is built on the mountainside

- The fire rages out of control and the boy with the birthmark vanishes. Presumably he has burnt to death. Despite the boys' good intentions, they are still immature and a danger to themselves

Part 2

Papering over the cracks
- The 'beast' is discussed at a meeting, unsettling all of the boys
- Ralph proceeds with his programme of improvements, helped by Piggy's intelligent suggestions. Shelters are built
- Jack becomes obsessed with hunting
- When the choir is meant to be tending the fire, Jack leads it on a hunt. The fire goes out and a ship passes by. Ralph is furious. Jack cannot challenge him but lashes out at Piggy – Ralph's brains – instead, breaking his glasses
- Piggy's glasses are a symbol of order. Breaking them undermines order on the island
- Ralph attempts to reassert his authority at a meeting. He says that the fire is of paramount importance
- Fear of the 'beast' persists. A hunt – Jack's area of expertise – is organised to kill it. Finding the parachutist moving in the wind, the boys are terrified. They decide that the 'beast' is real and avoid it

Part 3

The collapse of order
- Jack challenges Ralph once more
- Beaten a second time, Jack leaves to form this own 'tribe'
- Tempted by hunting and feasting and not having to work, many boys join Jack's savages
- The conch group continue to stand for order and fairness; the savages become a dark, erratic force
- Simon – bearing the truth about the 'beast' – is killed by the frenzied savage mob

- Piggy's glasses are stolen. When the conch group attempt to retrieve them, Piggy is killed and Sam and Eric are forced to join the savages
- Ralph, now alone, is hunted like a pig. He is no longer treated as a human. Only the naval officer prevents Ralph's death and the complete collapse of order

Conclusion   At first, the boys try to replicate the orderly environment they have come from. Partly due to their inexperience, and partly because of the malevolent spirit of Jack, their efforts are disjointed and unproductive. Jack and his savages become the dominant force on the island, subverting order wherever they find it. In the end they are even prepared to kill Ralph – a figurehead of order – and are only the intervention of the naval officer averts a complete collapse of order.

FURTHER QUESTIONS

Here are four more common questions on the novel. Work out what your answer would be, always being sure to draw up a plan first.

1 Examine the characters of Ralph and Piggy. Explore their relationship as it changes and develops through the novel.
2 Choose three or four dramatic events. Explain what happens in each and say how you think they might best be portrayed on film.
3 Compare and contrast the characters of Ralph and Jack. How do their characters affect their leadership styles?
4 Imagine that you are Ralph who, having returned home, is telling his adventures to his father. What might he include or leave out? (This could be written in script form.)

PART FIVE

CULTURAL CONNECTIONS

BROADER PERSPECTIVES

Many novels deal with similar themes to *Lord of the Flies*, as Golding was addressing universal problems. *Animal Farm* (1945) by George Orwell, for instance, is a satirical sketch of Communism at the time, as practised on a farm taken over by its own animals. An initial desire for fairness and democracy gets lost in the conflict between Napoleon and Snowball – two pigs – who in many ways resemble Jack and Ralph. Ultimately the ruthless and dictatorial Napoleon triumphs. An intelligent and far-sighted donkey, Benjamin, shares Simon's gift of prophecy.

The child's perspective has also been popular with novelists. *The Catcher in the Rye* (1951) by J.D. Salinger is a very personal and American view of adolescence at around the same time that Golding was writing *Lord of the Flies*. For an English outlook it is worth reading *Cider with Rosie* (1959) by Laurie Lee. The book recalls Lee's childhood in the Cotswolds during the First World War (1914–1918) and the Twenties, and provides an interesting comparison with Golding's depiction of the 'littluns'.

Golding drew on a tradition of adventure stories, many of which he had read and loved when himself a boy. A well known example, *Robinson Crusoe* (1719) by Daniel Defoe, involves Crusoe, the central character, being wrecked on a desert island. He is totally alone until a native – Man Friday – arrives. Crusoe's despair at his loneliness is reminiscent of Ralph's homesickness.

Peter Brook made a film of *Lord of the Flies* in 1963. He took a group of schoolboys to the Caribbean island of Vieques for three months and got them to act out the book with very little direction from Brook himself. The result is a powerful and atmospheric adaptation, very much in the spirit of Golding's novel. A second version of the film was made in 1990 by Harry Hook. It includes additional characters who are not in the original novel and is, therefore, less helpful for students of the text.

Another relevant film is Lindsay Anderson's *If...* (1968) which shows an English public school as its dissatisfied pupils stage an armed uprising.

allegory The depiction of a person close in character and behaviour to someone else who is usually seen in a different context. For example, Jack's dominant and power-hungry manner is often likened to that of Hitler; Simon's eccentricity and kindness are interpreted as Christ-like or akin to a prophet or visionary.

fable A simple story, often using animal characters, with a message or moral which can be seen in, or applied to, everyday life. The primary message, in the context of this novel, is that human beings are naturally capable of evil despite their outward appearance and conditioning towards good/civilised behaviour. (See Original sin below.)

hypallage Describing something as having a quality or property it cannot possess. For instance, Golding refers to 'the unfriendly side of the mountain' (p. 48). A mountain is inanimate and so cannot express friendship, although it may appear unwelcoming in some way. This is also known as a 'transferred epithet'.

image, imagery Images are pictures which help to give a greater understanding to the reader. They may be simple similes or metaphors, or more vivid and complex. Simon's cry that he had seen a dead man on a hill provides a direct image of Christ crucified on the hill at Calvary.

irony This can mean saying one thing and meaning something quite the opposite; it may also extend to situations in which one action mocks or ridicules another, when an ill-fated event leads to a more favourable one or vice versa.

metaphor Writers use various devices to help make their meaning clearer to the reader. Simple comparisons, or similes, can be useful; these are usually preceded by 'as' or 'like'. (For example, 'as cold as ice' or 'like a gust of wind'.)

Metaphors take the idea of comparison a stage further and describe things as if they had physically changed into something quite different. For instance, Golding describes the sea as a leviathan, or whale, endowing it with some of the qualities that the creature possesses.

onomatopoeia Some words sound like, and echo, the action they describe, for example 'splash', 'swish' and 'smack'. In *Lord of the Flies* words like 'Zup' and 'Pht' are used to convey the flight of a hurled stone and the sound of a spear.

original sin This is a Biblical reference to Adam and Eve in the garden of Eden, or Paradise, being tempted by the Devil. God would not forgive them and human beings were thereafter recognised as inherently sinful. They must strive and work to be good but being bad is their natural state. Some of the boys on the island revert to this state.

romanticism This is a vague and much abused term which, in the context of *Lord of the Flies*, has nothing to do with the subject of love. It refers rather to those things which are perceived in an unrealistic, emotional or idealised way. For example, both the boys and the naval officer have a 'romantic' notion of what life on the island could be like which is distinctly different from the reality. Ralph's understanding of himself; his innate sense of justice and decency and the supremacy of 'noble' thoughts and ideals in the absence of civilising influences could be viewed as 'romantic'.

subplot The main storyline of any novel is referred to as the plot; any additional story (usually of less significance) is termed the 'subplot'. In *Lord of the Flies* the main plot is what happens to the boys on the island and the two factions which emerge. What happens to Simon; his thoughts, ideas and behaviour as a separate individual, could be regarded as a subplot. Although the main plot and any subplots are different and distinct, it can be seen that they can be interrelated and mutually contribute to the overall action of the novel.

symbolism A symbol is an object or action that can represent ideas and events of wider importance; for instance the conch, glasses or 'beast'.

tri-syllabic chanting During and after hunting the pigs the boys take up a simple and repetitive chant. (*'Kill the pig. Cut her throat. Bash her in.'* (p. 82)). Each phrase contains three syllables or beats, the first and third being strongly stressed and the second, or middle syllable, being much weaker. The rhythm produced sounds like a military drum beating 'dum, dee, dum'.

TEST ANSWERS

TEST YOURSELF (Chapters 1–4)
A 1 Piggy (*Chapter 1*)
••• 2 Simon (*Chapter 1*)
3 Piggy (*Chapter 2*)
4 Jack (*Chapter 2*)
5 Piggy (*Chapter 4*)
6 Simon (*Chapter 3*)
7 Piggy (*Chapter 4*)

TEST YOURSELF (Chapters 5–8)
A 1 Ralph (*Chapter 5*)
••• 2 Simon (*Chapter 5*)
3 Maurice (*Chapter 6*)
4 Piggy (*Chapter 6*)
5 Jack (*Chapter 6*)
6 Jack (*Chapter 8*)
7 Simon (*Chapter 8*)

TEST YOURSELF (Chapters 9–12)
A 1 Piggy (*Chapter 9*)
••• 2 A savage – Jack? (*Chapter 10*)
3 Eric (*Chapter 10*)
4 Ralph (*Chapter 11*)
5 Jack (*Chapter 11*)
6 Sam (*Chapter 12*)
7 Jack (*Chapter 10*)
8 Simon (*Chapter 9*)
9 Ralph (*Chapter 12*)

NOTES

NOTES

Notes

TITLES IN THE YORK NOTES SERIES

GCSE and equivalent levels (£3.50 each)

Harold Brighouse
Hobson's Choice

Charles Dickens
Great Expectations

Charles Dickens
Hard Times

George Eliot
Silas Marner

William Golding
Lord of the Flies

Thomas Hardy
The Mayor of Casterbridge

Susan Hill
I'm the King of the Castle

Barry Hines
A Kestrel for a Knave

Harper Lee
To Kill a Mockingbird

Arthur Miller
A View from the Bridge

Arthur Miller
The Crucible

George Orwell
Animal Farm

J.B. Priestley
An Inspector Calls

J.D. Salinger
The Catcher in the Rye

William Shakespeare
Macbeth

William Shakespeare
The Merchant of Venice

William Shakespeare
Romeo and Juliet

William Shakespeare
Twelfth Night

George Bernard Shaw
Pygmalion

John Steinbeck
Of Mice and Men

Mildred D. Taylor
Roll of Thunder, Hear My Cry

James Watson
Talking in Whispers

A Choice of Poets

Nineteenth Century Short Stories

Poetry of the First World War

Forthcoming titles in the series

Advanced level (£3.99 each)

Margaret Atwood
The Handmaid's Tale

Jane Austen
Emma

Jane Austen
Pride and Prejudice

William Blake
Poems/Songs of Innocence and Songs of Experience

Emily Brontë
Wuthering Heights

Geoffrey Chaucer
Wife of Bath's Prologue and Tale

Joseph Conrad
Heart of Darkness

Charles Dickens
Great Expectations

F. Scott Fitzgerald
The Great Gatsby

Thomas Hardy
Tess of the D'Urbervilles

Seamus Heaney
Selected Poems

James Joyce
Dubliners

William Shakespeare
Antony and Cleopatra

William Shakespeare
Hamlet

William Shakespeare
King Lear

William Shakespeare
Macbeth

William Shakespeare
Othello

Mary Shelley
Frankenstein

Alice Walker
The Color Purple

John Webster
The Duchess of Malfi

Y

FUTURE TITLES IN THE YORK NOTES SERIES

Chinua Achebe
Things Fall Apart

Edward Albee
Who's Afraid of Virginia Woolf?

Jane Austen
Mansfield Park

Jane Austen
Northanger Abbey

Jane Austen
Persuasion

Jane Austen
Sense and Sensibility

Samuel Beckett
Waiting for Godot

John Betjeman
Selected Poems

Robert Bolt
A Man for All Seasons

Charlotte Brontë
Jane Eyre

Robert Burns
Selected Poems

Lord Byron
Selected Poems

Geoffrey Chaucer
The Franklin's Tale

Geoffrey Chaucer
The Knight's Tale

Geoffrey Chaucer
The Merchant's Tale

Geoffrey Chaucer
The Miller's Tale

Geoffrey Chaucer
The Nun's Priest's Tale

Geoffrey Chaucer
The Pardoner's Tale

Geoffrey Chaucer
Prologue to the Canterbury Tales

Samuel Taylor Coleridge
Selected Poems

Daniel Defoe
Moll Flanders

Daniel Defoe
Robinson Crusoe

Shelagh Delaney
A Taste of Honey

Charles Dickens
Bleak House

Charles Dickens
David Copperfield

Charles Dickens
Oliver Twist

Emily Dickinson
Selected Poems

John Donne
Selected Poems

Douglas Dunn
Selected Poems

George Eliot
Middlemarch

George Eliot
The Mill on the Floss

T.S. Eliot
The Waste Land

T.S. Eliot
Selected Poems

Henry Fielding
Joseph Andrews

E.M. Forster
Howards End

E.M. Forster
A Passage to India

John Fowles
The French Lieutenant's Woman

Elizabeth Gaskell
North and South

Oliver Goldsmith
She Stoops to Conquer

Graham Greene
Brighton Rock

Graham Greene
The Heart of the Matter

Graham Greene
The Power and the Glory

Thomas Hardy
Far from the Madding Crowd

Thomas Hardy
Jude the Obscure

Thomas Hardy
The Return of the Native

Thomas Hardy
Selected Poems

L.P. Hartley
The Go-Between

Nathaniel Hawthorne
The Scarlet Letter

Ernest Hemingway
A Farewell to Arms

Ernest Hemingway
The Old Man and the Sea

Homer
The Iliad

Homer
The Odyssey

Gerard Manley Hopkins
Selected Poems

Ted Hughes
Selected Poems

Aldous Huxley
Brave New World

Henry James
Portrait of a Lady

Ben Jonson
The Alchemist

Ben Jonson
Volpone

James Joyce
A Portrait of the Artist as a Young Man

John Keats
Selected Poems

Philip Larkin
Selected Poems

D.H. Lawrence
The Rainbow

D.H. Lawrence
Selected Stories

D.H. Lawrence
Sons and Lovers

D.H. Lawrence
Women in Love

Laurie Lee
Cider with Rosie

Christopher Marlowe
Doctor Faustus

Arthur Miller
Death of a Salesman

John Milton
Paradise Lost Bks I & II

John Milton
Paradise Lost IV & IX

Sean O'Casey
Juno and the Paycock

George Orwell
Nineteen Eighty-four

John Osborne
Look Back in Anger

Wilfred Owen
Selected Poems

Harold Pinter
The Caretaker

Sylvia Plath
Selected Works

Alexander Pope
Selected Poems

Jean Rhys
Wide Sargasso Sea

William Shakespeare
As You Like It

William Shakespeare
Coriolanus

William Shakespeare
Henry IV Pt 1

William Shakespeare
Henry IV Pt II

William Shakespeare
Henry V

William Shakespeare
Julius Caesar

William Shakespeare
Measure for Measure

William Shakespeare
Much Ado About Nothing

William Shakespeare
A Midsummer Night's Dream

William Shakespeare
Richard II

William Shakespeare
Richard III

William Shakespeare
Sonnets

William Shakespeare
The Taming of the Shrew

William Shakespeare
The Tempest

William Shakespeare
The Winter's Tale

George Bernard Shaw
Arms and the Man

George Bernard Shaw
Saint Joan

Richard Brinsley Sheridan
The Rivals

R.C. Sherriff
Journey's End

Muriel Spark
The Prime of Miss Jean Brodie

John Steinbeck
The Grapes of Wrath

John Steinbeck
The Pearl

Tom Stoppard
Rosencrantz and Guildenstern are Dead

Jonathan Swift
Gulliver's Travels

John Millington Synge
The Playboy of the Western World

W.M. Thackeray
Vanity Fair

Mark Twain
Huckleberry Finn

Virgil
The Aeneid

Derek Walcott
Selected Poems

Oscar Wilde
The Importance of Being Earnest

Tennessee Williams
Cat on a Hot Tin Roof

Tennessee Williams
The Glass Menagerie

Tennessee Williams
A Streetcar Named Desire

Virginia Woolf
Mrs Dalloway

Virginia Woolf
To the Lighthouse

William Wordsworth
Selected Poems

W.B. Yeats
Selected Poems

York Notes – the Ultimate Literature Guides

York Notes are recognised as the best literature study guides.
If you have enjoyed using this book and have found it useful, you
can now order others directly from us – simply follow the ordering
instructions below.

HOW TO ORDER

Decide which title(s) you require and then order in one of the following
ways:

Booksellers
All titles available from good bookstores.

By post
List the title(s) you require in the space provided overleaf,
select your method of payment, complete your name and
address details and return your completed order form and
payment to:

> *Addison Wesley Longman Ltd*
> *PO BOX 88*
> *Harlow*
> *Essex CM19 5SR*

By phone
Call our Customer Information Centre on 01279 623923 to
place your order, quoting mail number: HEYN1.

By fax
Complete the order form overleaf, ensuring you fill in your
name and address details and method of payment, and fax it
to us on 01279 414130.

By e-mail
E-mail your order to us on awlhe.orders@awl.co.uk listing
title(s) and quantity required and providing full name and
address details as requested overleaf. Please
quote mail number: HEYN1. Please do not
send credit card details by e-mail.

York Notes Order Form

Titles required:

Quantity	Title/ISBN	Price

Sub total _____

Please add £2.50 postage & packing _____

(*P & P is free for orders over £50*) _____

Total _____

Mail no: HEYN1

Your Name _____

Your Address _____

Postcode _____ Telephone _____

Method of payment

☐ I enclose a cheque or a P/O for £_____ made payable to Addison Wesley Longman Ltd

☐ Please charge my Visa/Access/AMEX/Diners Club card
Number _____ Expiry Date _____
Signature _____ Date _____

(please ensure that the address given above is the same as for your credit card)

Prices and other details are correct at time of going to press but may change without notice. All orders are subject to status.

☐ *Please tick this box if you would like a complete listing of Longman Study Guides (suitable for GCSE and A-level students)*

York Press

Longman

Addison
Wesley
Longman